Ravel

VLADIMIR JANKÉLÉVITCH

Translated by Margaret Crosland

Ravel

GREENWOOD PRESS, PUBLISHERS
WESTPORT, CONNECTICUT

Library of Congress Cataloging in Publication Data

Jankélévitch, Vladimir.
   Ravel.

   Reprint of the ed. published by Grove Press, New York,
which was issued as no. 3 of Evergreen profile books.
   Bibliography: p.
   Discography: p.
   1. Ravel, Maurice, 1875-1937.
[ML410.R23J22 1976]   780'.92'4 [B]   75-28925
ISBN 0-8371-8473-8

*The child's costume from 'L'Enfant
et les Sortilèges' (M. Terrasse)*

Originally published in 1959 by Grove Press, New York
and John Calder, London

Reprinted with the permission of Grove Press, Inc.

Reprinted in 1976 by Greenwood Press
A division of Congressional Information Service
88 Post Road West, Westport, Connecticut 06881

Library of Congress Catalog Card Number 75-28925
ISBN 0-8371-8473-8

Printed in the United States of America

10 9 8 7 6 5 4 3 2

Ravel
by Vladimir Jankélévitch

Contents

Costume for the Cat from
'L'Enfant et les Sortilèges' (P. Colin)

Development

'I can feel his heart beating.'
(Maurice Ravel speaking of a mechanical chaffinch[1])

Maurice Ravel attained perfection with prodigious rapidity
Like his teacher Fauré and to some extent like Chopin, Ravel
found his true self almost at once. Not that one cannot see reflected
in his work the successive phases of literary sensibility from 1890
onwards, traces of the influences he underwent, and even the tricks
of fashion; at the end of the last century it was Chabrier, Satie and
the Russians, including a certain *fin de siècle* languor which soon
left him; later, during the productive years between 1905 and the
war, came the return to Couperin; after the war, jazz, Stravinsky
and polytonality. And yet, in spite of its changing faces Ravel's
art does not reveal the exaggerated sensitivity of Debussy's art; it
was evident from the start that this young man would be more
strong-minded and less receptive than Debussy. No influence can
claim to have possessed him entirely; new styles seem to have
aroused in him more technical curiosity than receptivity, modifying
his way of writing but not his language, leaving no more trace
behind than an occasional chord, a trick of instrumentation or a
peculiarity of spelling: for although he was so rarely impressionable his ear was miraculously sensitive and he had an almost
unlimited appetite for what was unheard, valuable and rare; but
these are pursuits which involve only harmonic sensitivity and not
the mental quality of emotion. Just as Debussy reveals himself as
impressionable and susceptible to the slightest shifts and the most
fleeting variations of taste, Ravel remains watchfully elusive
behind all the disguises due to the snobberies of the times.

---

[1] Quoted by René Chalupt, *Ravel au miroir de ses lettres*, p. 259.

Yet he was not made of marble; he too responded to the most imperceptible currents in painting and poetry: symbolism, impressionism, cubism, the Russian ballet, Mallarmé, Henri de Régnier and Léon-Paul Fargue... the delicate antennae of his music could capture everything.

This music was immediately lucid and clearly conscious of its own purpose. Lucid rather than precocious, it is free of those legendary anecdotes which usually build up the hagiography of child prodigies; unlike those infants of mythological times, Ravel neither strangled two boa-constrictors in his cradle nor composed a concerto when he was three; altogether he was something of a bad scholar and it is well known that his failure in the Concours de Rome occupies a memorable place in the list of the Institut's bad errors of judgment. However, Debussy's success proves that submission to the conventions of cantata is not entirely incompatible with the audacity of genius. It is true in fact that Debussy groped much more among the temptations of facility; Debussy learnt only slowly how to deny pleasure and the desire to please, before choosing the strait and narrow way... Ravel on the contrary went immediately straight to the goal, as though possessing the infallible foreknowledge of formal perfection. His hand never wavered. It is only too easy to forget that the Habanera in the *Rhapsodie espagnole*, with its astonishing changing notes, dates from 1895.

1895 was a miraculous year, the year of the *Cinquième Barcarolle*, the year when Fauré was no doubt already contemplating *Prométhée*, when Debussy was working on his *Trois Nocturnes* for orchestra and playing the first fragments of *Pelléas* on Pierre Louÿs' harmonium. Incomparable years which made Paris into the musical capital of Europe again... In that year Ravel was twenty. In the works that he composed up to 1900 it may be possible to recognise some preferences and models, even quotations. First of all Ravel certainly loved Massenet; Ravel listened to the melodious sirens of pleasure: for youth was not always as austere as it is today. We know furthermore what attraction Manon and Charlotte had for Monsieur Croche,[1] and what expressions he found to celebrate the grace 'of clear complexions and whispering melodies'. He would have admitted what we would have guessed all the same, merely by listening to the Clair de lune from the *Suite bergamasque* or the second *Ariette oubliée* which asks 'What is this languor?'... The reasons for the discredit into

---

[1] *Monsieur Croche antidilettante*, p. 85. (An essay by Debussy. Tr.).

which Massenet has fallen include not only our understandable distaste for facility but also, we can be sure of it now, a grudge against our own pleasure, the masochistic enjoyment of boredom, the cult of false profundity and a sort of inverted frivolity which is very common in contemporary salons... How can Ravel's hard music owe something in its turn to Massenet's coy phrases, which are so soft, approximate and sensuous that even young women, for whom they were written, today prefer *The Art of Fugue*? Massenet represents all that is easy-going, facile and relaxing, the very opposite to the sharp clear-cut music of Ravel. He did not come willingly to the lyricism of opera nor to theatrical display in general, and for us he is the incarnation of honesty, humour, and the laconic attitude; sometimes his harmonies bite. But what if this spitefulness were only the ambivalent mask of tenderness? If we examine carefully the development of Ravel's melodic line between the *Menuet antique* of 1895 and the Concerto of 1930 we may possibly encounter, suppressed in shame, the voluptuous arabesques and caresses of Massenet.

It must be said that the severe fasting to which Ravel subjected himself formed the regular régime of his master Gabriel Fauré. In 1896 in fact Fauré succeeded Massenet as professor of composition at the Conservatoire. According to Roland-Manuel this class of Fauré's offered to composers what Mallarmé's salon offered to poets, 'a magic place favourable to free discussion', and the class taught Ravel the power of pianissimo and the eloquence of reticence. Apart from a subtle *Berceuse* for piano and violin Ravel dedicated to Fauré the Quartet in F major[1]; then there is the grace of *Lydia*, with its additional streak of acidity, which hovers gracefully round the tender melodic line and envelops the notes with the delicate light of its minor key. And then there is *Le Jardin féerique*, which is a very close relation to the *Dixième Nocturne* and the noble Epithalamium from *Shylock*. Minuets, madrigals and pavanes create a bergamask background for the two composers, a background of *fêtes galantes* with the eternal Clitandre and all the figures of carnival. *Le plus doux chemin* and the intermezzo of the girl flute-players in the first act of *Pénélope*, the *Madrigal* in D minor and the *Pavane* in F sharp mark out a line of development which Gounod had already followed in *O ma*

[1] Read again the charming pages that Ravel wrote on *Clair de lune* in the special number of the *Revue musicale* devoted to Fauré (1921–1922, p. 24–25). On the influence of Fauré, cf. *l'Heure espagnole*, p. 107 and *Valse* (piano solo), p. 13.

belle rebelle, and apart from Ravel's *fêtes galantes* some very Fauré-like pages of Messager were to follow the same path. This is *le plus doux chemin* of bergamask charm. No-one is taken in by the climate of twilight and affectionate irony, and above all by that allusive, entirely muted speech. All of it comes to Ravel from the sweet, inexhaustible, melodious river of music and song that flows calmly through the thirteen barcarolles like a river of honey. Ravel lived in the aura of magic which emanated from Fauré for nearly half a century; it is fitting therefore to associate from the very first the composer of *Le Secret* with the name of the man who was the most secretive, the most deeply disguised, the most fiercely modest artist that France has known since Racine.

In composition class with Fauré.

After supreme distinction comes truculent clowning, for one of the principal sources of Ravel's music can be found in Chabrier. This name will seem even more surprising than that of Massenet; it is strange to find an affinity between Chabrier, the man who was self-taught, who was so vital but so terribly unequal, and the subtle artisan of the *Trio*, who was always so attached to formal perfection; or an affinity between the supercilious and slightly patrician humour of *L'Heure espagnole* and the broad comedy of *L'Etoile*. Imagine the Punch of the *Joyeuse Marche* entering like a thunder clap, roaring with laughter, turning somersaults, with all his little bells ringing; this vulgar creature, with his truncheon, his false nose, his hump back and the two vermilion patches on his

Chabrier by E. Detaille (1887)

cheeks would soon have broken all Adélaïde's[1] porcelain. What is the connection between this good-natured 'comic' and the slightly acid humour of the mischievous Ravel, and since when did exuberance go hand in hand with modesty? But perhaps there is no cause for this confusion. Does not Fauré, the most refined artist in the world, think of Chabrier in *Le Pas espagnol*? Without mentioning Spain, which they both loved to the same extent, Ravel owes to Chabrier first and foremost the idea of a purely musical pleasure that has no connection with literature.[2] Chabrier, fully launched into music, resembles one of those demons of farce mentioned by Kierkegaard, 'sons of caprice, drunk with laughter and dancing with joy'[3]; with instinct as his one infallible guide, stimulated further by an exceptionally delicate sense of hearing and an insatiable appetite for novelty, he experimented before anyone else with all sorts of delectable combinations and he put notes together for the exclusive pleasure of the ear. The Ravel of 1899, when he risked this phrase so reminiscent of *Gwendoline*:

had no wish to write parodies. The pirates in *Daphnis et Chloé*, *Tout gai*, the *Chanson à Boire* and the exuberant Rigaudon from *Le Tombeau de Couperin* are hardly less lively than the *Joyeuse Marche*. Indeed Ravel denied the uncontrolled Chabrier influence in *Pavane pour une infante défunte* or in the *Menuet antique*, twin brother of the *Menuet pompeux*; for Chabrier, as a general rule, wrote down everything that went through his head, pouring out indiscriminately the brilliant and the bad, astounding discoveries and fairground tunes, the most penetrating poetry and the most scandalous bad taste, everything, too, with the same generosity, for this volcanic nature was never capable of selection. How was it that an artist as honest and scrupulous as Ravel was not shocked by this bric-à-brac where Valkyries rub shoulders with café-

---

[1] *Adélaïde* was the ballet adapted from *Valses nobles et sentimentales*. (Tr.)
[2] Igor Stravinsky has expressed in glowing terms his sympathy for Chabrier (*Chroniques de ma vie* v. 1, p. 43).
[3] *Repetition.*

concert songs? How could he survive this régime of violent contrasts in which platitudes and the most discouraging vulgarity in the melodic ideas alternate with exquisite refinement? We should read again the parody which Ravel wrote, without malice, in 1913, 'in the manner of Emmanuel Chabrier': in this way the kind Séverac,[1] beneath the rose-laurels, becomes good-naturedly gay at the expense of the *Scherzo-Valse*.[2] In particular he reproaches the exaggerated baroque quality of the expression, the style with its everlasting appoggiaturas and grace notes, the slightly over-complex basses, and this sentimental unison of the two hands playing a few octaves apart, as in opera, to double the melody and catch at the listener's heart-strings. But his mockery indicates also his preferences: antique modes, leading note sevenths and dominant ninths ascending in parallel lines towards the climax, these clear sonorous notes, so French and so full of the future, and this sudden incursion into F sharp major which like a whim suddenly passes through the *Faust* waltz; at this point parody becomes homage paid to the son of delirium, caprice and liberty. Clear, graceful ninths, unresolved ninths, juxtaposed for the mere pleasure of the senses! In 1887 French music experimented delightedly with them, first in those three *Sarabandes* where Erik Satie approached them without preparation, handled them from all angles, delighting in their cool sonorities, in turn silvery or strangely hieratical, then later in the prelude to *Le Roi malgré lui* with its pealing notes which seem to be the fanfares of the free open air and the wide sky. On the other hand the *Habanera* of 1895 doubles the melody in the same way as Chabrier's *Habanera*. And further, without the second *Valse romantique*, the seventh *Valse noble et sentimentale* would perhaps not exist. Neither, without *España* and the *Scherzo-Valse*, would the Feria in the *Rhapsodie espagnole*.

Ravel hardly had time to know Chabrier, who died in 1894; on the other hand he was a contemporary of the early eccentricities of Satie, his intuitive genius, and his dangerous prospecting in the no-man's land of harmony. Monsieur Pierre Daniel Templier recalls[3] how Ravel insisted on playing himself

[1]   Joseph-Marie Déodat de Séverac, 1873–1921. A native of Languedoc, he was noted for his 'impressionist' style of composition, and his early death was a great loss. (Tr.).

[2]   *Sous les lauriers-roses*, p. 15–18.

[3]   P. D. Templier, *Erik Satie* (collection Rieder, 1932), p. 32–33. ('He assures me, every time that I meet him, that he owes me a lot. I am very pleased', said Satie of Ravel.)

at the S.M.I. in 1911 some of Satie's youthful compositions, including the second *Sarabande* (which was in fact dedicated to him) a *Prélude du fils des étoiles* (of which he made an orchestration, still unpublished) and the third *Gymnopédie*. No doubt the composer of the *Sites auriculaires* also passed through his esoteric period and wrote in a 'flat style' at the precise moment when Erik frequented *Le Chat noir* and *Le Sar péladan*; a melody written in 1896, *Sainte*, based on Mallarmé, with its procession of dreamily juxtaposed impassive chords is just as reminiscent of the *Sonneries de la Rose-Croix* as of *La Damoiselle élue*. The *enchaînements* in the Prelude to *L'Heure espagnole* derive perhaps from there. The fascination which casts a spell over the immobile *Gibet* and bewitches the monotonous *Boléro* is perhaps not unconnected with the obsession of the *Gnossiennes*. As for the faltering succession of dominant ninths aligned in the *Pavane pour une infante défunte* and *Manteau de fleurs*, or the minor ninths in the *Vocalise-étude*, their origin is clear; they derive from the mournful and precious languor of the euthanasia which undermines the *Sarabandes*. Debussy was to remember it in the ninth movement of his suite *Pour le Piano*. 'My sister, can you not hear something dying?' But it is to be noticed that in *Serre d'ennui* (1896) Chausson also admitted the magic of these sonorities.[1]

---

[1] *Serres Chaudes* by Maeterlinck, op. 24 (recueil Rouart, p. 35, 36, and Franck, Hulda III). Cf. Debussy, *Pelléas et Mélisande*, act V (p. et ch. p. 292). Ch. Koechlin, *Poèmes d'automne* op. 13, No. 2: *Les rêves morts* (p. 12–13, 17). Darius Milhaud himself unceasingly juxtaposes these ninths in the *Sept poèmes de Paul Claudel extraits de la Connaissance de l'Est* (1912–1913).

14

These languid successions and sonorous ninths were to be heard again in the first of the Clément Marot *Epigrammes*, and even in the *Asie* from *Shéhérazade*.

Ravel is noticeably more artistic, more resourceful and less restricted than the Silenus of Arcueil. Soon he, the pioneer, the explorer, the pathfinder, was to come as an elderly scholar to learn from Ravel.[1] Yet Ravel never ceased to be faithful to him[2]. even in the fanfare from *L'Eventail de Jeanne* (1927) where the ironic description 'Wagneramente' reminds us of the 'Chaldean *Wagnérie*'; for Satie and Ravel are brothers in humour as they were formerly in languor and hermeticism. It is possible that the macabre fantasmagoria of *Gaspard de la nuit* owes something to the author of the *Danses gothiques*, the lover of castle keeps and turrets in bronze. Satie and Ravel were so jealous in their modesty that they were afraid of being taken in by all that they cherished most in the world; this is why Chabrier, gently ill-treated in the 'Paraphrase of *Faust*', also serves Satie as a target in *Españaña*. It is true that Chabrier had parodied Wagner just as Satie and Ravel parodied Chabrier, and the impertinent *Souvenirs de Munich* ('Fantaisie sur des thèmes favoris de Tristan') look forward both to the *Golliwog's Cake-walk* and the Fauré-Messager *Quadrille tétralogique*. It is possible to go further: Ravel shared with Satie the same non-conformist and fiercely independent spirit which kept him apart from honours and decorations and

[1] See in *Satie* by P.-D. Templier (engraving 28 communicated by Darius Milhaud), an analysis of *Le Noël des jouets*.
[2] Roland-Manuel, *Maurice Ravel et son oeuvre* (Durand, 1914) p. 9. The same author (*A la gloire de Maurice Ravel*, p. 30, 33, 35; Revue musicale 1925, p. 18; *Maurice Ravel et son oeuvre dramatique*, p. 77) calls the walk from *La Belle et la Bête* the 4th *Gymnopédie*. Ravel dedicates to Erik his 3rd *Poème de Mallarmé*, *Surgi de la croupe et du bond*; Erik to Mme. Joseph Ravel his 2nd Description automatique, *Sur une lanterne*.

from attachments to women; it was that spirit which made him so hard to know and so disturbing.

Learning again the taste for liberty from Satie, and confidence in his own pleasure from Chabrier and Fauré, Ravel found in the Russian school inexhaustible food for his curiosity concerning modes, rhythm and harmony. One can imagine the astonishment of the French composers, after 1880, at this violent poetry, in turn dreamy and wild. It is not surprising that the bells of *Boris Godounov*, *Ivan the Terrible* and *Prince Igor* sounded the retreat to the evil gods, the black moths and all the Nibelung nonsense. Ravel in his turn, motivated by this characteristic hunger for novelty, discovered with delight the voluptuous indolence of the slavonic melodies; something of this went perhaps into the *Beaux oiseaux du Paradis* where the modal key of F minor and the returns to tonic unison evoke a kind of Russian nostalgia. The pedal-work and the lovely chromatic colour of Borodin's work fascinated him, and although Ravel laughed at them in the Waltz 'in the manner of Borodin', the young girls from *Prince Igor* and the shadow of 'Notturno' from the Second Quartet can sometimes be felt haunting his work. Neither can it be proved that the pirates' dance and the final Bacchanal from *Daphnis et Chloé* do not owe something to the whirl of a famous Polovtsian dance. They may reveal a discordant and slightly mischievous Borodin. These agile pirates are more closely related to the Tartars of Borodin than to the heavy Wagnerian Danes of *Gwendoline*. Ravel owes to Balakirev[1], as to Liszt, certain daring qualities in his pianism – for *Islamey*, along with *Thamar*, is one of the delightful origins of French revival, the elder sister of *Ondine* and the *Alborada del Gracioso*. To Rimsky-Korsakov Ravel owes the subtlety of the orchestra, the colour of the timbres and the instrumental virtuosity. The subtle French *Shéhérazade* bears little resemblance to the four brilliant symphonic pictures by Rimsky-Korsakov, but Ravel's use of the orchestra, like Dukas' use of it in *La Péri*, certainly derives from the *Capriccio espagnol*. The cadences in the Prelude to Night and the sweeping strokes on the harp in the Feria from the *Rhapsodie espagnole* are certainly linked to Rimsky-Korsakov's *Shéhérazade* and it is hard to say why,

---

[1] It appears that in the Prelude to *Myrrha* (1st Cantata by Ravel which won a prize at the Concours de Rome in 1901) a theme for cellos and double basses is based on Balakirev (C. Photiadès, in *Revue de Paris*, 1938, I, III, p. 221).

Rimsky-Korsakov.

from the very beginning of *Asie*, the melody for the right hand makes one think irresistibly of *Antar* and its fragile 'Arab melody'.[1] Even in the Adagio from the Quartet there are certain throbbing demisemiquavers which do not deceive and reveal clearly their Russian origin. Just before the third part of *Daphnis et Chloé* certain alternations of tonality are reminiscent not only of *Ivan the Terrible* but of *Boris Godounov*. For more than any other composer Ravel enjoyed Mussorgsky. Like *Pelléas* he enjoyed the fresh, acidulated and astringent flavour of the consecutive seconds which bring those prickly crumpling sounds to *La Chambre d'enfants*. In *Noël des jouets*, the *Histoires naturelles*, the

---

[1] *Shéhérazade*, version for piano and voice I, p. 6: 'I should like to see the lovely silk turbans....'; and *Antar*, 4th part. Cf. Debussy, *En sourdine*.

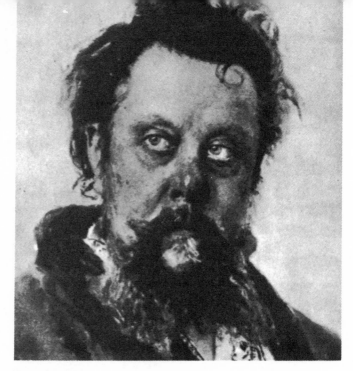

Mussorgsky.

scene with Father Arithmetic in *L'Enfant et les sortilèges*, we find again that minute precision of notation, this taste for detail, this capricious lack of continuity in the speech, this microscopic realism in fact which characterises the composer of genius who wrote *Pictures from an Exhibition*. But Mussorgsky wrote like this from instinct, Ravel did so as a civilised man, through extreme study and industry. It should be remembered that Ravel instrumentalised the *Pictures from an Exhibition* and fragments from *Khovanchtchina*. *Scarbo* from *Gaspard de la nuit* seems a reincarnation of the *Gnomus* from *Kartinki* and the staccato passages in *Nicolette* are reminiscent both of those from the *Gopak* and of the humour in the *He-Goat*. Ravel remembered for a long time the escaped parrot in the fifth act of *Boris*, the appearance of the automaton and the bell-ringing scene. The sharp music of the

18

bird ballets and insect concerts[1] was to fill Ravel's fairy stories *Ma Mère l'oye, L'Enfant et les sortilèges*, for a long time: just as they were to fill the humming garden of Albert Roussel. Even an interest in Hebraism was shared by Ravel and Mussorgsky; and just as Ravel confronts *Kaddish* and *L'Enigme éternelle*, Hebrew prayers and Yiddish songs, the Old Testament and Mayerke, so with Mussorgsky, *Josué* and the Song of Songs shouldered with Samuel Goldenberg and the Jews in the Sorotchintsi ghetto.

Most of all Ravel resembles Liszt. The orchestra of the *Rhapsodie espagnole* and *La Valse* bears the closest resemblance to the marvellous orchestra of the *Mephisto Waltz* and the *Faust Symphony*, so modern even then, so violent, metallic and elastic. Ravel had discovered in the *Twelve Transcendental Studies* and the *Three Concert Studies* a treasure house of technical, harmonic and sonorous novelties. The crackling of the *Feux Follets*[2] appears again in *Scarbo*; the *Waldesrauschen* comes to life again in the capricious fluttering of the *Noctuelles*. *La Vallée des cloches* with its countryside angelus and its romantic Swiss background seems to come from a Year of Pilgrimage. The *Jeux d'eau* murmur at Versailles just as at the Villa d'Este. The unparalleled qualities of Liszt's *Poèmes Symphoniques*, the crystalline sonorities of *St. Francis of Assisi preaching to the Birds*, and the non-conformism of the Studies find a successor in Ravel. Maurice Ravel sees himself, if not always in the spirit of romanticism, then at least in the spirit of audacity and liberty that Liszt, the rhapsodist and the ultramodernist, represented for French composers. The *Rhapsodie espagnole* and the *Hungarian Rhapsodies* of the romantic genius find an echo in the *Tzigane* and the *Rhapsodie espagnole* of the French composer.

---

[1] The Daddy long-legs and the Flea from *Boris*, the Cockchafer in the *Enfantines*, the Chickens from the *Pictures from an Exhibition*, the Magpie.... With Ravel, the Cricket from the *L'Histoires naturelles*. Also remember the Prologue to *The Snow Maiden*. For the influence of Mussorgsky, cf. again *Daphnis*, p. 67–68 (end of the 2nd part); *l'Enfant et les sortilèges* p. 15. Cf. an article by Ravel on *Boris* in *Comœdia illustré*, 1913.

[2] Cf. Mendelssohn, *Capriccio brillante*, op. 22.

19

I. 1875-1905

Ravel's first stylistic period includes three works for the piano: the *Menuet antique*, *Pavane pour une infante défunte* and *Jeux d'eau* (the first two are orchestrated); vocal works (four melodies, and above all *Shéhérazade* for voices and orchestra); finally the String Quartet in F Major (1902) which introduces the period of greatest mastery.

The *Menuet antique* (1895) is a fairly insignificant and rather conventional work. It could almost be said that the 'Menuet pompeux' from Chabrier's *Pièces pittoresques* contains more spontaneity and goodness of heart. From the *Menuet antique* to the subtle *Menuet sur le nom d'Haydn* and the minuet from *Le Tombeau de Couperin* the distance is certainly as great as from the *Pavane* to the *Alborada*, that is, from the Spain of Hugo to that of Manet. The *Menuet antique* can hardly owe its title to the fact that it contains no leading notes. The fact is that F sharp minor will not tolerate an E sharp (and accepts even a G natural), and C sharp will not tolerate B sharp. But these are only nice little

20

details. The modulations seem timid and the composer draws things out somewhat. But there is no need to turn up our noses. The trio in the middle, with its delightful C natural, possesses a graceful naive quality that is by no means ordinary; the cadences in this trio, if they did not come to a wavering finish with a traditional close, might sometimes contain a presentiment of the Forlane in *Le Tombeau de Couperin*. The Ravel of *Adélaïde* appears also in certain delightful chords that the orchestra entrusts to the harp and the strings (plus one note sounded on the small flute). They look forward to the skilful and slightly sentimental grace of the *Menuet sur le nom d'Haydn*.

Adélaïde   *Menuet sur le nom d'Haydn*

It is worthwhile listening to the whole of the *Menuet antique* for the sake of these tricks, repeats, graceful acknowledgements and *badinage* with high notes. The *Pavane*, although it was written later (1899), can hardly be defended; its three variations are somewhat tedious and it is impossible to find any personal accent in it.[1] The famous *Jeux d'eau* (1901) on the contrary, is a work full of imagination, and of the three it is certainly the most astonishingly masterly, both through the originality of its style and its evocative poetry. Fragile fourths and fifths float lazily beneath the limpid arpeggios in the right hand; these clear, crystalline, transparent sonorities create an atmosphere which is related at the same time to the romanticism of Liszt, the impressionism of Debussy and even more so to the enchantments of Gabriel Fauré's *Ballade* in F sharp, although it remains specifically Ravelian. The harmony, with its discordant bass, its changed outlines, its chromaticism and even a hint of bitonality, forms sometimes a curious prelude to the inventions of *La Péri* and *Firebird*. Yet it cannot be said that *Jeux d'eau* is not dated; there is repetition and more relaxation also than in *Miroirs*; the tender second subject which languishes on the black

[1] *L'Esthétique de la grâce* by Raymond Bayer contains a detailed analysis of the *Pavane*.

21

keys, the doleful and weary mood of an autumnal heart in *Le grand parc solitaire* is certainly a very decadent and crepuscular landscape for the creator of *Adélaïde*.

It was however the same background that he evoked in his first song, *Sainte* (1896), to some precious and slightly Carlovingian words by Stéphane Mallarmé. The atmosphere of this slow procession of chords is reminiscent (if only through the dominant sevenths and ninths) of Debussy's Third *Prose lyrique*, *De fleurs*, with its perfect chords juxtaposed in a liturgical manner in several keys. It is impossible also not to think of the *Oraison* from Chausson's *Serres chaudes*, Charles Koechlin's *Prière du mort* and the Rosicrucian, 'gothic' hierarchism of the early Satie. Maeterlinck's 'blue boredom' and Debussy's 'green boredom' correspond. In Ravel's music, between the chords, the voice sings a kind of litany which floats dreamily in the middle register evoking Clymène in her glory, rather than Adélaïde. The effect is not unlike a stained glass window, yet all the same there is a touch of ingenuity in the line of the song that is already ironic. Let no one be mistaken. This Clymène does not signify so much languor as mystery, a finger at her lips, smiling and impassive... what surprises does she hold in store? The unresolved ninth which ends the melody opens on to infinity and nowhere, and promises all those surprises that the sphinx announces for us. The game has become quite apparent in the two charming *Epigrammes de Marot* (1898); in the first, *D'Anne qui me jecta de la neige*, which evokes the pomp and splendour of a Renaissance court, and in the second particularly, *D'Anne jouant de l'épinette*, with its graceful clavichord tone. The first is perhaps the more ceremonious, employing the solemn

D'Anne, qui luy iecta de la Neige.

Anne (par ieu) me iecta de la Neige,
Que ie cuidoys froide certainement:
Mais c'estoit feu:l'epperience en ay ie,
Car embrasé ie fuz souddainement.
Puis que le feu loge secretement
Dedans la Neige, ou trouueray ie place
Pour n'ardre point? Anne, ta seule grace
Estaindre veult le feu, que ie sens bien,

and slightly faded key of G sharp minor (the relative key of B) which was the key used later for the Second Greek melody; and the other, a charming ritournelle, proceeds on its own little way in C sharp minor,[1] and ends curiously enough on the same chord of G sharp, that is to say on the dominant. One can imagine the mysterious clavichord player in the Vermeer portrait reeling off on the spinet, with her agile fingers, the 'soft and melodious sound'. On the other hand *Manteau de fleurs* (1903), all sparkling with sharps and brilliant ornaments, is a return to a richer, more opulent and more generous tonal medium. Adélaïde was certainly to speak the language of flowers more soberly. The piece should be judged by its lively harmonious finish, with its great harp arpeggios with their closely packed notes through which vibrates the sixth degree, for the 'augmented sixth', here as well as in Séverac's music, resounds in the vertical thickness of the chord. The voice 'sings' a great deal here and the colour of F sharp major envelops all the notes warmly. That same Anne who, when she played the spinet, already let us hear the Prelude to *Le Tombeau de Couperin*, no longer wishes to be frivolous and takes herself seriously again. Already one can foresee the 'indifferent' from *Shéhérazade*.

Shéhérazade (1903), is a kind of symphonic poem for voice and orchestra, a lyric work of greater scope yet one in which everything conspires to date both the style and the artistic approach; the wanderlust of the *Voyage d'Urien* seems to impregnate every note. Listening to this serious declamation, so free, so open and full of song, it is hard to go on believing Ravel's music is dry. *Asie*, the first of the three *Shéhérazade* poems, and by far the longest, consists of a succession of varied episodes placed between a prelude and a re-exposition; these episodes correspond to the successive ports of call of a *bateau ivre*, a 'bark on the ocean' which is carrying out its great oriental tour; in this way the archipelagos and the exotic seas pass by before the eyes of the new Sadko. The exordium begins with a magnificent cascade of major sevenths which fall from the heights among the boiling foam and cracklings of phosphorus and finish in a kind of barcarolle above which can be heard distant ringing notes, like the call of the open sea and of legendary promontories; two fifths stretch beneath the caravel of desire their moving depths of

[1] Arthur Hoerée, *Les Mélodies et l'oeuvre lyrique*, in the *Revue musicale*, special number devoted to Ravel, 1st April 1925 p. 48.

concordant discords; then follow, in turn, in the bass, the mystical sonorities of *La Damoiselle élue*, in the treble, punctuated by the celesta, staccato fifths and fourths which prepare us for the Chinese touches in *Laideronnette*; finally, after a fortissimo which takes hold of the entire orchestra, the echo of the opening calls dies out slowly in a kind of luminous mist. A common idea seems to possess *Asie* and *La Flûte enchantée*, ensuring the thematic unity of this rhapsodic voyage[1]. The idea already haunted the Scherzo of the Quartet. *La Flûte enchantée* is a delightful serenade in which Ravel allows the god Pan's instrument, the syrinx, to sing; Daphnis was to recount, later, how it was invented, the flute that belongs to Bilitis, the Faun, the Little Shepherd and the Girl with the Flaxen Hair, to all the slender, lily-like creatures of the symbolist spleen. One day Ravel was to enjoy speaking a more incisive language; but in the counterpoint which half way through the piece confronts the sonorous trills in the slave girl's song, there is already great flexibility. In *L'Indifférent*, to end, the key of E major and the slow drum-beats create a tonal medium that is even more voluptuous; the melodic lines are very close together, and the overlapping fifths and fourths envelop the melody here in a heavy sensual atmosphere. Such is this glittering piece of orientalism, which contains no irony, and where the slave girls have not yet learnt the modesty of their feeling. *Shéhérazade*, with its cataracts of short notes, reveals itself to us from the start as extremely melodious and entirely ornamented with trills, arpeggios, tremolos and glissandos. Yet it can be said that Tristan Klingsor's words 'to interrupt the story artistically' awaken in Ravel a bad conscience about facility; in this respect the narrative with the repeated notes curves modestly downwards and already announces the recitative of *Le Martin-pêcheur*.[2] And most of all the singing phrase from *L'Indifférent* is certainly an echo from the Quartet.

The String Quartet in F major[3] (1902) dominates, with its youthful grace, all the production

---

[1] Version for piano and voice, p. 7 and 15 and p. 18-19.
[2] *Histoires naturelles* (in the words: 'has come to place itself there'). *Shéhérazade* p. 15.
[3]. Cf. the themes on p. 189.

Drawing by Ravel on the back of a chair at Montfort-l'Amaury.

of this period. Ravel therefore began where the other composers finished, the others being Franck, Chausson, Fauré and Smetana. Ravel's precocity gives the lie to Vincent d'Indy's aphoristic statement that a string quartet is necessarily a work of maturity. At the time of the Quartet Ravel was twenty-seven; and it is true that Debussy was barely over thirty when he wrote his; but Ravel's Quartet is much more typical of its composer than Debussy's. Ravel's Quartet is a beginning, while Fauré's Quartet, in its austere colourlessness, is a terminus and a last thought, *opus ultimum*. We can distinguish, in the order of their appearance, nine principal motifs which make up the melodic substance of the Quartet. A naive and straightforward phrase (A) rises gradually to the upper register – simple, docile black notes and quavers attached to a single scale of fifteen notes which spans two octaves (from F to F) during the first four bars and then, with the fifth bar, in a sudden pianissimo, descends the other side of the slope in A minor and ends on the chord of G minor. Could there be anything gentler and lighter than this tone of F major? It is indeed the same fine, subtle and almost Mozartian atmosphere of the Capriccio in Gabriel Fauré's *Pièces Brèves*; there are the same feather-light pianissimos and the same appearance of tranquillity. And there is also the same limpid writing, the same subtly articulated polyphony as in Glazounov's delightful Second Quartet op. 10 in A major. This poetry is affectionately normal. However, perhaps we may be wrong, there is already a hint of atticism behind so much juvenile artlessness. Perhaps the secret lies in the slightly capricious teasing of the melodic line with its flat levels and its A–E fourths, the innocent doubling of the second note of the A theme, or perhaps in some surprising change of key that no modulation led us to expect? Is it rather the effect of certain harmonic repetitions and continuity, sudden crescendos and decrescendos which seem to correspond to the breathing of the phrases? Or perhaps the secret is revealed in this expressive and imperceptibly arch idea (B) which assumes a smile from the ninth bar onwards through its subtly changing harmonies? In any case these delightful things certainly show a desire for exterior amusement and pleasure for the ear. The third theme, which is very expressive, is distinguished by its triplet, singing as in the first theme, with its characteristic gruppetto of two quavers in duple time; and the rest of the development consists mainly in the opposition of these two themes, C being developed above the first notes of A, then A above C;

25

twice running the counterpoint is reversed in this way, and the intervention of B in its turn leads to a most powerful fortissimo which begins the re-exposition and the coda. The Scherzo, although it has less brilliance than the Spanish Scherzo in Debussy's Quartet, plays skilfully with dubious rhythms; it sets out three themes of which the first two (D and E) are obviously related to C; as for F, the type of slow intermezzo which serves as a Trio counterpoints it first with E and then with D, at the same time that the repeated notes betray its close kinship with A. A dreamy Andante, in the midst of which A reappears, but a calm, serene and melancholy A, develops in its turn two motifs (G and H) in G flat major; A, entwined with a very energetic rhythmic formula, hesitates and feels its way both at the opening and close of the Andante, in a capricious kind of improvisation. After a moment of passionate exaltation which announces *Daphnis et Chloé*,[1] the 'Dumka', ever thinner and more distant, goes higher and dies softly away. The Finale, with its tapping bows and its slight chromaticism opens like a well-known Finale by Franck; to the two principal themes of the first movement (A and C) and their variants, a last motif (I) is now added, with a delightfully innocent air which gives a hint of the Sonatine and *Ma Mère l'oye*. This perpetual speed, these semiquavers, these octave tremolos as well as a certain preoccupation with decoration all accentuate the impression of divertissement and the desire to be superficial which an over-sentimental Andante had almost obscured. The Menuetto from Joseph Jongen's[2] delightful *Sonatine* was to recall, along with the Minuet in Ravel's *Sonatine*, the initial idea of the Quartet.

---

[1] *Daphnis* (piano solo) p. 33.
[2] *Sonatine* (1929), II

II. 1905-1918

The incomparable period lasting from the *Sonatine* to *Le Tombeau de Couperin*, that is from 1905 to the first world war, does not correspond to a regular and continued evolution in Ravel's style: for instance the *Introduction et Allégro* for harp, which belongs to 1906, is much behind the *Sonatine* and could belong to the *Shéhérazade* period; on the other hand Mallarmé's *Poèmes* (1913) already give a hint of the post-war style, and so do the *Valses nobles* (1910), although they were written before *Le Tombeau de Couperin*, which by contrast seems to be contemporary with the *Sonatine*. The Quartet, as far back as 1902, was the master-stroke. Unlike Fauré therefore, who went forward gradually and always in the same direction, Ravel was masterly and infallible at the age of twenty-seven and from then on he was to profit from whatever came his way.

During these ten years Ravel's vocal work comprised twenty-six melodies, including choral works, one *Vocalise*, harmonised

27

popular songs and two groups of songs, the *Histoires naturelles* and Mallarmé's *Trois Poèmes*. The *Noël des jouets* (1905) is a little stiff, in spite of its stylistic finesse, its fragile resonance, and repeated notes, its pianism that is already ingenious and the lyric ardour suddenly awakened by the words *Du haut de l'arbuste hiémal...* The pathetic gusts of the *Grands Vents venus d'outremer* (1906) form a violent contrast to this juvenile collection. There is nothing particularly Ravelian in this stormy poem, neither the entirely romantic chromaticism of the style nor the strong concerted basses so close in expression to Debussy's *Poèmes de Baudelaire*. The melody begins like the first movement of a sonata and ends with a ninth above which lolls a C natural – the sixth – looking onto the open sea and the infinite horizons of nostalgia, and remaining unresolved. One day the *Valses nobles et sentimentales* were to require from Henri de Régnier pretexts of a quite different kind, no longer this background of roaring ocean swell, but the idea of a delectable pleasure well sheltered from storms. And then in 1906 came the five *Histoires naturelles* and their chattering flock of birds, their carnival of animals, their farm-yard full of cheeping, chattering, and scattered feathers; first of all *Le Paon*, the Peacock, a kind of wedding march in a comically pompous rhythm which already announces all the majesty of the Concerto for the left hand; while on their side the chords which spread out their tails, glissandos which dazzle by their contrary movements on the black notes, look forward to *L'Heure espagnole*, which was in preparation at the same time.

Design by Toulouse-Lautrec for 'Les Histoires Naturelles'.

After the strident 'léon' cry of this noble fowl comes the delicate insect trotting of *Le Grillon*, the Cricket. With its augmented fifths, ninths and major sevenths, and its harmonic elevenths, the Cricket in its own way prepares the way for *L'Heure espagnole*; this can be judged from these two descending successions:

The G sharp of the fragile transposed beats becomes dominant in the key of D flat major, and it is also in this key that Ravel ends, after a contemplative and dreamy coda in which nocturnal chords offer poetic contrasts to the capricious cricket; the tall silent poplars pointing to the moon represent here the same vertical suggestion as 'the tall slim fountains among the marble statues' formerly represented in Fauré. There is a very different and at first entirely impressionist atmosphere in *Le Cygne*, the Swan. Here the septuplets of demisemiquavers, fluid arpeggios imbued with haze and pedalling, the sprightly key of B major, everything brings to this song a kind of luminous mist reminiscent of *Shéhérazade* and *Jeux d'eau*. Fauré's Swan[1] gliding over the limpid pool would certainly cause less foam and sparkle. In Ravel's song the harmonies float like white clouds between sky and water, to rhythms frequently uneven, within which septuplets are set against basses in duple time, surrounding the notes with a kind of fluffy mist which blurs all the outlines. But while at the end of *Le Grillon* the fun came to an end in the nocturnal peace of a solemn perfect chord, here, on the contrary, fun chokes the undulating arabesques; the liquid arpeggios dry up; brief chords, unkind, tired and prosaic, an incisive recitative, strong, sharp, prickly rhythms overlay the cloud of pedalling. *Le Martin-Pêcheur* (the Kingfisher), with its huge accumulations full of closely packed notes and its strange rustlings, seems to evoke some Debussyist autumn.[2]

---

[1] *Cygne sur l'eau* (Mirages, No. 1), 1919.
[2] *Feuilles mortes* (Préludes, IIe. Cahier).

Here again, for the third time, *L'Heure espagnole* can be seen coming to maturity:

After the mysterious eclogue comes a bomb explosion, with a discordant note – the cackle of *La Pintade* (the Guinea-Fowl); these discordant sevenths, which come as though in anger, without any preparation (G sharp next to G natural, A natural next to A flat), were to fill the *Alborada del gracioso* with their caustic sounds. In this song the repeated notes, the aggressive staccatos, the biting, sliding sounds create a kind of turbulence as far opposed to the pomposity of the Peacock as to the tick-tock of the Cricket.

After these five animal silhouettes there came, in 1907, a *Fête galante*, and a *Vocalise*, an exercise in vocalisation. *Sur l'herbe* is the single encounter between Ravel and a poet who inspired Debussy and Fauré to so much divine music. Perhaps Verlaine's unpaired lines and abandon did not suit our severe artisan. Yet he did not dislike Watteau, with his minuets and picnics. Whatever the case, beneath the insipid mandoline arpeggios, the disjointed gallantries, licentiousness and affectation one can detect music that is strict, and perfectly conscious of its intentions. From 1907 onwards Ravel pursued a new line of development through exoticism and folklore. This is clearly visible first of all in the *Vocalise* in the form of a Habanera with its nostalgic and obsessive Andalusian melody, which is almost contemporary with the *Rhapsodie espagnole* and *L'Heure espagnole* (with its closing Quintet that contains the same flowery ornaments); finally it is most visible of all in the harmonisation

30

of the *Cinq Mélodies grecques*.[1] First comes the graceful *Chanson de la mariée*, in its harmonic dress that is so discreet and subtle – clear octave beats in triplets of semiquavers, sustaining throughout the song an obstinate tonic bass; *Là bas vers l'Eglise*, a marvel of reticence and sobriety in its mauve dress of G sharp minor; the delightful *Chanson des cueilleuses de lentisques*, permeated by its hypolydian D sharp, its soft accents and a delicately insistent augmented sixth. *Quel galant m'est comparable* supplies a contrast to the slightly melancholy charm of these three songs through its harsher light and the candour of a simple recitative interrupted by a sort of peasant refrain through which one seems to hear the shrill sound of fifes; *Tout gai* has an accent almost as direct, with its symmetrical verses and its square 2/4 rhythm which is slowed down in places by a bar in 3/4 time; the composer of the *Joyeuse Marche* would certainly not have denied this return to the living origins of joy!

The *Quatre Chansons populaires* which won a prize in 1910 in the Competition of the 'House of Song' in Moscow belong to the same vein; their monotonous verses, their vitality and spontaneity betray their folk origin. First comes the *Chanson espagnole*, with its strongly pronounced modal flavour; although Ravel has written so much better in this genre, it is still worth listening to these little refrains for the guitar which appear in D minor and resemble improvisations, with their chords of packed notes, their muscular arpeggios, their sharp timbres and their arid staccatos; next, the *Chanson italienne*, and it is hard to believe that Ravel harmonised it seriously, for the Roman seriousness of this *canzone* is such a far cry from the Guinea-Fowl and all the mischievous birds. C minor, the key of romantic pathos... And what exaggeration there is also in this pompous gruppetto of demisemiquavers in the ultra-conventional cadences, and the violent contrasts between *piano* and *forte*. However, it is impossible to be more concise – this Roman song is indeed the quintessence of emphasis, the greatest concentration of pathos. Spanish melancholy and Italian grandiloquence give way, in the *Chanson française*, to that sovereign clarity and luminous charm which could be described as the prose of the heart. Everything is orderly and ravishingly light-hearted; instead of minor keys we now have the everyday C major, C major as

---

[1] To which is now added a 6th melody, posthumous, (*Tripatos*) written for Mlle. Marguerite Babaïan who kindly showed us the manuscript in 1939.

transparent, friendly and familiar as a little-season afternoon in the provinces: a few chords, fourths and sixths, the most normal intervals, a waltz rhythm, as quiet as the smoke of a little town rising straight up into the blue sky... any moment we could start thinking of Du Bellay, La Fontaine and distant memories of childhood. After this delicate Loire sky the heart contracts a little at seeing next the violent oriental colour of the *Chanson hébraïque*, which is interrupted, after each stanza, by a kind of liturgical psalm based on solemn perfect chords. It is interesting to compare with this song the two magnificent *Mélodies hébraïques* which date from 1914 and were made famous by Madeleine Grey.[1] First is the fervent *Kaddisch*, the prayer for the dead, with its pathetic melody in C minor, over a bass in G; the prayer deepens with rapid broken chords which could belong to the harp, while the voice, with almost fanatical exaltation, declaims its ecstatic *vocalises* over strange clusters of notes. *L'Enigme éternelle* is distraught, anxious and slightly cynical, limping along with all its dissonances (A sharp and D sharp in E minor), opposing to Biblical hieraticism the plebeian clumsiness of its Yiddish jargon. By some miracle of intuitive sympathy Ravel entered deeply into that mixture of humour and bitterness that makes up the Jewish type of anxiety.

The *Trois Chansons* for mixed choir (1915) might belong rather to the background of songs from the Limousin district. *Nicolette* is certainly not a sad song, although it is a trifle cynical: a theme followed by three 'variations', the Wolf, the Page, graceful and ethereal, the rich Barbon (cousin to Don Iñigo, no doubt, and suitable for inclusion in the gallery of elderly admirers) tells us the story of the bad Little Red Ridinghood; in the fourth verse we can distinguish the comic discords which announce the elderly beau and the capricious changes of style allowed to the spontaneous fantasy of the story; one note for each syllable, as a rule, as in the *Chansons populaires*, and particularly in the cheerful *Ronde*, where young men and girls converse with the old men and women. Of the three settings the most refined and at the same time the most prophetic, is the *Trois beaux oiseaux du Paradis*, an exquisite ballad full of tenderness; its imponderable harmonisation, transparent style and humble linear quality cut across the slightly exterior petulance of the *Ronde*. Just as the Peacock

---

[1] The *Trois chants hébraïques* by Louis Aubert (1925), *Kol Nidrev* (in Hebrew), the moving *Berceuse* and *Der Rebele* (in yiddish), dedicated to Madeleine Grey, seem to be influenced by Ravel.

The 'driver' Ravel at the front.

in the *Histoires naturelles* looked forward to Iñigo Gomez in *L'Heure espagnole* the Birds of Paradise look forward to the perfect sympathy of *L'Enfant et les sortilèges*. And finally, although it belongs to 1913, a group which looks to the future even more than the *Trois beaux oiseaux du Paradis*. The *Trois Poèmes de Mallarmé*, written for the voice and various instruments (two flutes, two clarinets, string quartet and piano) reveal Ravel's predilection for small chamber ensembles that was to express itself later in the *Chansons madécasses*. Of the three poems *Soupir* is the most impressionist, with its streaming arpeggios of demisemiquavers, clearly related to the septuplets of *Le Cygne*. From 1901 therefore, the year of *Jeux d'eau*, until 1913, the same cult of fluidity is developed through *Le Cygne*, *Une barque sur l'océan* (1906), *Ondine* (1908), and the Sunrise from *Daphnis et Chloé* (1911). The melodic line however already possesses qualities of clarity, hardness and incisiveness which do not deceive: the decadent languor of the 1890's is definitely over. This is still more clearly visible in *Placet futile*, in which the precious gallantry might recall *Sur l'herbe* if the melody was not sometimes cruelly incisive; this progress in a way indicates the entire interval which separates the voluptuous abandon of Verlaine and the fine hardness of Mallarmé. Ravel's music has now grown its teeth; to the fluid poem *Surgi de la croupe et du bond* the composer brings the vibration of limpid, merciless resonance made stranger still by the high register of the keyboard, the discordant basses and the aggressive superimposition of tonalities.

In the five years between 1905 and 1910 Maurice Ravel enriched the literature of the piano with some of his most accomplished chefs-d'oeuvres. The earliest of them, the *Sonatine*, is exquisitely and divinely successful. It is a 'Sonatine' first of all – like those by Roussel and the six delightful *Sonatines* by Novak – through its modest dimensions, for it has three movements instead of four; secondly and above all through its style, which is very much the style of the Marot *Epigrammes*, purposely fragile, and except at the end of the Minuet, deprived in its low notes of the powerful support of the bass. A naive melody in F sharp minor cuts across the chord of C sharp almost immediately and flies away gracefully to the beat of demisemiquavers fluttering in the twilight sky of F sharp. There are sudden pianissimos, delicate colourings and ravishing moments of warmth. As in the Quartet, a hint of lightheartedness, an imperceptible smile mingles with the shuddering melancholy. The smile can be surprised in the

34

delicate fifths without bass, in the false naïveté of the repeats with their delicate accents brought out by the left thumb like pealing bells, and even in the limpid thirds of the close.[1] The Minuet in D flat, which has been interpreted as a 'colloque sentimental' between two shadowy figures from Verlaine,[2] offers in contrast to this gentle liveliness a serenity that is more pompous and more solemn. Through a cyclic coquettish fancy found again in the Quartet, the final divertissement, written in the style of a toccata,[3] brings back the naïve melody of the first movement; a recollection of this melody was already apparent in the few slower bars which served as trio for the Minuet; finally it emphasises this scintillating descending succession of perfect major chords in several keys at the end of which the key of F sharp major gleams again, in golden effervescence.

If the Sonatina is related to the chaste ingenuousness of the Quartet, the five images which make up the suite entitled *Miroirs* (1906) belong to the impressionist heritage of *Jeux d'eau*. It is a fine, most powerfully poetic picture book, full of dream, with its seascapes, bird-calls, misty landscapes and distant sighing guitars in the warm Andalusian night. *Noctuelles* is a poem of fluidity; everything here is fusion, gliding, liquefaction; over the ground strewn with leading notes move the great butterflies of twilight in heavy zig-zag flight, beating their wings and wandering like blind birds through the evening air. Loosened rhythms, resonance that is now misty, now crystalline, and then cloudy trailing chromaticism as in Liszt's *Waldesrauschen*. In Ravel's piece everything is seeking, groping, escaping. The outlines however are already more acid and glittering, the skill is harder than in *Jeux d'eau*. The melancholy of *Oiseaux tristes* is certainly of a more static kind. There everything was flight, chase and pursuit; now the bird-call lingers between two *roulades*, then hangs discordantly over moving basses; this dreamy E flat becomes temporarily D sharp and lingers in this way to the end above multiple lines freely superimposed on each other; the writing is just as disjointed as that of *Barque sur l'océan* appears fluid and continuous. For here now is the praise of arpeggios: the flowing barcarolle, with its broken

[1] For this conclusion, compare *La Belle et la Bête* (ballet score p. 23), *Une barque sur l'océan* (*Miroirs*, p. 31), *Vocalise*, *Sur l'herbe*, *Prélude* for piano.

[2] A. Cortot, *Cours d'interprétation*, edited by Mme. Jeanne Thieffrey, p. 171.

[3] Note (p. 12) a sentence which Gabriel Dupont recalls in *La Maison dans les dunes*.

chords over which float fifths, fourths and seconds, evokes the great lullaby of the ocean and the rocking of a boat which sails up and down the troughs of the waves. This writing has a great deal of pedal and is very molten, enveloped in softness like the Allegro for harp; then in violent contrast comes the dryness of the *Alborada del Gracioso*. Here Ravel carves his lines hard and deep, and the pedal mist is dispersed, leaving the incisive and arid staccatos completely bare; after the big waves, the foaming swell, the gusts of arpeggios, come the brief arpeggios for guitar. There are various elements here: first the dance theme proper, in D minor, which in the orchestral version is divided between the harps and strings in pizzicatos, playing hide and seek with itself; in these furtive imitations, the true accent is often lost; second, there is a protean motif which is reduced to a triplet of demisemiquavers, assumes all types of disguises and abandons itself to all kinds of frolics; third, the expressive solo of the recitative (entrusted to the first bassoon in the instrumental version) which breaks into the middle of the Aubade and wraps sinewy vocalisations round huge clusters of hurried notes; this recitative, comparable to the trio of a scherzo, plays the same role as the Tonadilla in Granados' pieces. At the end the theme of the recitative hammers out its notes like fanfares below the principal motif in harsh discords. The last image in this Mirror, *La Vallée des cloches*, is certainly also the oldest,[1] as can be realised from the romantic atmosphere of the background, just as much from the intensely lyric melody, a forerunner of *Daphnis et Chloé*, which flows in full spate between a double row of major seconds. *La Vallée des cloches* pays homage to fourths; the erratic bass of the *Oiseaux tristes* returns – here there is a G sharp suspended from loose rhythms, around which the right hand embroiders a pattern of dreamy fourths; against this misty background soft discords soon emerge – E natural, G sharp – floating insistently, lingering like distant sounds in the depths of the valley; and to ensure that nothing is lacking from the 'very much Séverac' atmosphere of this poem, a quiet chanting is heard next – perfect chords in F sharp around which the fourths from the beginn-

---

[1] Is it a new version of the 2nd piece of the *Sites auriculaires*, 'Entre cloches', which remained unpublished? M. Cortot (*La Musique française de piano*, v. II, p. 36 and 27) affirms this; Roland-Manuel (*A la gloire de Ravel*, p. 42) formally denies it.

ing cling obstinately, rising gently like the Angelus in this motionless twilight. In contrast to the incisive design of the *Alborada*, *La Vallée des cloches* seems to indicate a cult of vagueness that Ravel had certainly renounced as far back as 1906.

The interval from 1906 to 1908 spans the entire distance that separates the shameful Debussyism of *Miroirs* from the profoundly personal language and the astonishing mastery of *Gaspard de la nuit*. The first of the three pieces, *Ondine*, is a marvellously expressive effusion unfolding under a shimmering tremolo of demisemiquavers; seven sharps in the key-signature, and showers of arpeggios everywhere. Ondine is the siren singing in the untold flowing springs. What imaginative force there is, and above all what precision in stroke and arpeggio, and what progress in strength since the early time of *Jeux d'eau*! The muscular tension imposed by the pianism of *Ondine* is only relaxed to give way to the nervous tension of *Le Gibet*; here the bell no longer rings for the angelus, as in the peaceful valley of *Miroirs*, it is the melancholy passing knell of the hanged men, 'plus becquetés d'oiseaux que dés à coudre'; diabolical conglomerations have taken the place of the calm evening songs and the floating bass of *Oiseaux tristes* has in its turn become as rigid as an iron bar. *Scarbo*, the wicked gnome, is the counterpart to *Ondine*; the thousands of waterdrops are followed by showers of sparks, and the last spray has not yet evaporated before the Scherzo begins, prickly with a kind of electric dryness, cat-like shudderings, nervously repeated notes, and sudden movements of violence. Two opposed and hesitant themes can be sensed, following the opening improvisation, in the alternation of three low ascending notes (A) and a tremolo in D sharp (B) – and a dominant bass which hisses in a discordant juxtaposition with the D and the A of a chord with a changing note belonging to A major. Once the scherzo has begun, the passionate, almost romantic A theme ascends and descends with big strides like an imp with long thin hands, while the B theme, leaping in anger, chokes any kind of development.

As a reaction against the harmonic complexities and the rich chords of *Gaspard de la nuit*, the suite *Ma Mère l'oye*, written for four hands in 1908 and transformed into a ballet in 1912, reveals a first effort to attain that simple linear quality which, following Satie's austere monody, was to be more and more sought after in post-war compositions. The five short

37

pieces which compose the suite for piano are preceded, in the instrumental version, by a *Prélude* and a *Danse du rouet*, and punctuated by interludes. The overture offers us, as it should, an undeveloped sketch of all the motifs in the score: first come juxtaposed fifths below which rings out a kind of miniature fanfare, which could be called the metamorphosis theme, for it is found again among the various tableaux and at the end of the Apotheosis; above these fifths there appears first of all a transposed harmonisation of the Pavane, then the Tom Thumb theme, and finally, in the bass, in a lingering discord, the muttering of the Beast. The opening fanfares, which echo each other at intervals of a fourth, calls which answer each other in canon, compose together a kind of tuneful cacophony very similar to the prelude to *L'Heure espagnole*. After the *Danse du rouet* begins, in the bass, the Pavane, which this time is not for a dead infanta but for a sleeping beauty, whose century-long sleep is gently lulled by chimes within. The distant legendary resonances which veil this lullaby may be due to the entirely Gregorian flavour of its cadences, or to the discreetly insistent bass in D, sub-dominant to the key of A, or perhaps to the unadorned voices in duet. It is difficult to know to what we

can attribute the charm of this melody which is as childlike as it is refined. Next comes the waltz of the sleeping beauty, but first in quavers in 6/8 rhythm; after various tremolos and glissandos which embellish this invitation to the waltz, the graceful 'Conversations' begin. The reluctant Beast approaches in the bass with his heavy triplet of quavers.[1] The Beauty theme appears in the treble, in F sharp, strident and transposed by terror, above the amorous roar of the Beast, whòse declarations become more and more passionate, until the fortissimo which unites the counterpoint of reconciliation; here the theme of the Beast, now pacified, appears in

---

[1] Cf. F. Mompou, Suburbis II, p. 12.

Beast's costume for
'Ma Mère l'oye'. (L. Leyritz)

an easily-flowing triplet beneath the Beauty's melody. A long ascending glissando – the enchantment is ended, the magic spell gives way, while the dramatis personae separate. The chromatic triplet, turning into the Prince Charming triplet, fades away in the upper register and then gives way to the Beauty theme, played more slowly until amorous semiquavers replace it. Then comes the *Petit Poucet* (Tom Thumb) theme; after various orchestral marvels, glissandos, tremolos, horn calls, here come the little, fragile well-behaved thirds marking out the trail of bread crumbs; they go upwards in scales which grow longer and longer like lost children walking two by two, holding each other's hands and groping to find their way. It is the idea of the second act in Louis Aubert's charming work *La Forêt bleue.* This *Gradus ad Parnassum* is naïve and poetic. Hardly have the children disappeared into the forest before a cadence on the harp, followed by a cadence on the celesta, begins the ballet of the curious toys and *chinoiseries*; tinkling over the black keys, like Debussy's *Pagodes*, the miniature march from *Laideronnette* has a truly 'Chinese air', just as Satie's *Tyrolienne* has 'a very Turkish atmosphere'; one day the tea-cup in *L'Enfant et les sortilèges* was to speak Chinese again, just as charmingly; the intermezzo, with notes of longer value, is developed with canon-like imitations and sings with a tender melodic line through which it is not difficult to recognise the persuasive voice of the Quartet:

In conclusion an ingenious counterpoint embroiders over this expressive melody the fragile chimes of the *Pagodes* and *Pagodines*. The theme of the metamorphoses, ringing out below a reminiscence of the Pavane, announces the awakening of Florine, the sleeping beauty. Now everything is ready for the transformation of the *Jardin féerique*; C major, free of its modulations, like real life freed of its night-time dreams, C major, so serious, simple and noble, illuminates all the calm glory of this apotheosis; intervals which are almost concordant, an affectionate melody which Séverac was to remember *sous les lauriers-roses*[1], and while the C and the G of the peroration

---
[1] For this Déodat de Séverac style, see also *Alborada* (*Miroirs*, p. 43; for the orchestra, descending arpeggio for clarinet).

40

ring out for twelve bars, the enchantment finally resolves into a benediction amid the triumphal blaze of glissandos and fateful fifths.

The *Valses nobles et sentimentales* (1911) possess qualities that are strangely hard, acid and clear, transparent and angular, preparing definitely the period of the Mallarmé *Poèmes*; the waltz, which is the most passionate and expressive of all dance forms, composes in this instance valuable figures for divertissement; with Liszt and Chopin the waltz was laden with all the ardours of the soul, but with Ravel the tender waltz reveals sharp harmonies, all prickly with stalactites and fine needles. The first waltz is frank and very energetic, settling firmly into G major on a dominant seventh with appoggiatura where E sharp resounds harshly instead of F sharp, while A sharp, C sharp and D sharp,[1] belonging to a chord of F sharp major with its sixth (D sharp), form a 'false relation' in conjunction with the D natural of the bass. No formality, no prelude of little notes or useless bars. With its symmetrical conduct and its clear impassivity, this waltz anticipates the Rigaudon in *Le Tombeau de Couperin* and the two pieces have in common the persistent qualities, the strongly emphasised cadences which resemble low bows, and even these vast accumulations of ninths, chords of five notes composed of four fourths piled on top of each other. Through the discords, the major seventh and the side-note, a kind of electric circulation is established all through these pages; Schubert's *ländler*, which seem to be the origin of this waltz, become distorted and sidetracked behind harsh rubbing sounds. The first Waltz is more 'noble' than 'sentimental', and the second more 'sentimental' than 'noble'; this sentimental colloquy between Adélaïde and Lorédan prolongs the love duet between Beauty and the Beast. The third Waltz, in E minor, (relative minor to the opening key) is particularly exquisite, and it is a delight for the pianist to rediscover, beneath the curtain of fragile notes and the 'language of flowers' the skilful naïveté of Liszt's three *Valses oubliées*, but also the Bergamask charm of Fauré. We can feel that the third Waltz and the subtle dance of Lyceion in *Daphnis et Chloé* are almost contemporary. The fourth piece is much more like a waltz, with its lively triple time, its

---

[1] For the interpretation of these harmonies, cf. Roland-Manuel, op. cit., p. 86, and Alfredo Casella, *L'Harmonie* in the *Revue musicale*, quoted number 1925), p. 36.

unexpected modulations, its flexible and sinuous plan with the major sevenths which are occasionally reminiscent of Darius Milhaud's *Saudades do Brasil*. The great composer of Liège, Joseph Jongen, was perhaps to remember the fourth Waltz in his *Valse gracieuse*.[1] The fifth (in E major) is a slow waltz full of insidious rustling. Energetic and nimble, with its fluid appoggiaturas, the sixth Waltz (in C major) describes wide circles, rises and falls, languishes occasionally and rests on basses in counterpoint with their ambiguous duple accentuation[2]; the choreographic version informs us at this point that Adélaïde, a worthy cousin of Nicolette, has despised her beloved friend for the sake of the duke's jewels. But everything is to be sorted out and the seventh Waltz explains misunderstandings: as a form of transition and also as an invitation to the waltz, it begins with a short prelude in the form of an improvisation in which the cadence of the sixth Waltz, going through three modulations, dies away on a C bass; then begins the waltz, deriving from Gabriel Fauré's *Valses-Caprices* its graceful animation, its passionate tenderness, and in the bass, the slyness of its accents. It has an airy, delightful vivacity. No musical ear could fail to recognise here the left hand of Fauré and the lightness of Debussy. Indeed 'les fées sont d'exquises danseuses'... From time to time certain violent moments foreshadow the great *Valse choréographique*, noticeably the fortissimo which bursts out after an irresistible crescendo, at the moment when the whirling couples can finally be seen beneath the chandeliers. It is curious to compare these compositions with the opening of Chabrier's second *Valse romantique*, which occasionally modulates capriciously into E minor. In order to cause a surprise the composer, in the middle of a waltz, introduces a grating little bitonal intermezzo with a strident, spicy harshness which must have horrified the listeners of 1911. In the Epilogue the remnants of the seven waltzes linger in torn shreds, the fourth first of all, then the sixth, (once in quavers, once in semiquavers), the first twice, far away in the bass, as though the clear chords were now only a mysterious whispering: the third, in C minor, and finally the second. A few more flutterings, progressively limper and

[1] *Petite Suite pour piano* (1924), No. 4. Cf. Turina, op. 47, no. 5 (*Contes d'Espagne II*, *Promenade*).
[2] In the orchestral version the 3/4 beats are paired, alternately, according to the 3/2 and 6/4 rhythms.

limper, in the mist of the great chords, above an obsessive tonic pedal; G finally dies away in its turn like F in the *Entretiens de la Belle et de la Bête*, and nothing remains of the madness of this night, except a little dew and the bitter mist of morning.

Ravel's chamber music, between 1905 and the war, consists only of an Allegro for harp and small instrumental ensemble, and the sublime *Trio*. The *Introduction et Allégro*, written for harp accompanied by string quartet, flute and clarinet (1906), takes us a long way back to the melodious, facile and brilliant style of *Manteau de fleurs*. Here again, as in *Asie*, is the deluge of shimmering arpeggios. It is true that the instrument lends itself to them. Glissandos come easily to the harp, and so do arpeggios. The melodic outline itself submits willingly to a kind of soft sentimentality which Ravel was soon to despise in favour of less rewarding sustenance. Yet this is still a graceful piece of concert music, quite equal to Debussy's seductive Rhapsody for Clarinet in B flat, with its crystalline resonance and the undulating liquidity of its virtuosity. The exordium, which is a kind of dreamy improvisation, has two themes: A, in major thirds, suspended with light grace between heaven and earth, moves by intervals of a fifth alternately ascending and descending; A is set out a second time one tone lower, and later on supplies the theme for a slow dance. B, which is reduced in the introduction to simple triplets of quavers, is to furnish the central development in G flat; sometimes in the expressive melody it unfolds there is a reminiscence of Tristan Klingsor's *Indifférent*. C, which only appears later, seems to have been developed successively below and above a slower version of B. The development reaches its climax in a great concert solo during which the harp plays pompously B, then A, among headlong glissandos and soaring chords. This solo leads normally into the re-exposition and the final divertissement, in which C and B build up the dance rhythm by degrees. If the harmony in this work were not entirely concordant and diatonic, one might catch a glimpse from time to time of the bacchanalian rejoicing of *Daphnis et Chloé*.

There is as much progress between the cheerful Quartet and the Trio (1914) as between *Miroirs* and *Gaspard de la nuit*. It is true that through the piano alone the *Trio* already surpasses, in symphonic power, the charming fourfold badinage with the violin bows in the String Quartet. The *Trio* is incomparably tauter, more striking also, more controlled; it is a radiant masterpiece of maturity. The plan for the construction and cycle is also less apparent than in the Quartet. There are no themes common to all four movements and continually modified or developed; the four parts are independent, and reveal an exceptional prodigality of melody. Over a bass in E, dominant of A minor, the piano, alone at first, and then echoed by the strings, sets out a delicate tune which is made even lighter still by its ambiguous rhythm and its thin chords of three notes; two stanzas, theme and counter-theme, which resemble the two faces of the song, occupy in this way twelve bars of the exordium. Theme A modulates into F, changes key and turns into a second theme (B) with a soothing rhythm and a coy naïveté that recall the Pavane from *La Belle au Bois dormant*; the violin in A, then the cello in D, set out this theme, at the end of which, in the low notes of the keyboard, there is a faint echo in the left hand of A: it could be described as the muffled steps of distant dancers beating the turf, during the night-time, with felted sandals. Sometimes the strings are doubled at an interval of two octaves, and this spacing creates real orchestral resonance; sometimes they exchange the A theme with the left hand above the arpeggios in the right hand. The re-exposition, which is cut short, goes into a sublime coda in which the first theme, becoming more and more distant and mysterious, dies away gradually in the key of C, relative major to the opening key. The dazzling Pantoum[1] takes the place of a Scherzo here. Three essential themes, one as wicked as Scarbo with its repeated notes and cruel staccatos, the other almost romantic, and the third, developed from the first in long, most expressive note values, are hurled against each other in an aggressive divertissement where the shattered chords, the hard insistence and the pitiless rubbing sounds cause showers of sparks to fly more than once. In contrast to these exploits, which make the *Valses nobles* look pale, the Passacaglia, in the form of a Largo, recalls the noble seriousness of *Anne qui me jecta de la neige*; a tune which is almost solemn swells and develops gradually from the left hand to the cello, then to the violin; it culminates in the middle of the piece where its gruppetto of two semiquavers stands out strongly after cadences

[1] A sung declamation in Malay, accompanied by instruments. A description given to poems such as *Harmonie du soir* by Baudelaire, where the 2nd and 4th line of each verse act respectively as the 1st and 3rd line in the following verse.

45

which are very reminiscent of *Ma Mère l'oye*; and then it becomes progressively plainer until it reaches again the linear simplicity of the opening statement. After this 'homage to Rameau' there comes, serving as Finale, a long Rondo theme, its rhythm based on an uneven bar and adorned with agitated luminous tremolos. This cheerful theme with its two symmetrical slopes is interrupted so that the piano may intone a sort of triumphal paean around which the strings play a scintillating trill in C sharp. The magnificence of these fanfares and parallel perfect chords juxtaposed in various keys, together with the general key of A major, end by giving the Trio a violent picturesque colour and an exuberance which form a total contrast to the subdued tones of the Quartet in F.

For the first time in 1907 Ravel approached the orchestra directly with the *Rhapsodie espagnole*. An obsessive design of four descending notes – F, E, D, C sharp – with discordant mysterious seconds floating beneath it, expresses in *Prélude à la nuit* the lassitude of a hot evening. All the 'perfumes of the night', as in Debussy's *Ibéria*, all the feverish poetry that Manuel de Falla breathed in near midnight in the gardens of the Generalife have mingled here their emanations and their nocturnal languor. There are pianissimos shimmering like a midsummer night's dream, and penetrating poetry in this rhythm which whirls like a spinning top in the depths of the Andalusian night, and in this fragile conclusion which lingers indolently on the sixth degree. The *Malagueña*, a dance in triple time from Malaga, which serves as a Scherzo, is rhapsodic in appearance, for it is very free and rather loosely put together with its perpetual changes of atmosphere; first comes a very rapid dance in three-four time with deep pizzicatos; second, a theme which quickly slows down in F sharp minor (then D sharp) in which the repeated notes have a guitar-like resonance and the cool sevenths a deliciously acid taste; third, a voluptuous recitative, comparable to the 'Copla' from the *Alborada*, in which the triplets, like the fluted outlines of an adaptable 'vocalise', slow down the *Malagueña* with a more confidential effusion; fourth, the four lunar notes of the Prelude which float dreamily between the Copla and the rapid conclusion. It is known that the miraculous Habanera from the *Sites Auriculaires* (1895) serves as andante to this rhapsody; even today one can hardly tire of admiring the nostalgic grace of these huge broken chords which lead us to expect their resolution into G or C, come up against a sustained dominant pedal – C sharp, and then against E in A major (relative of F sharp), and flow back limply, leaving a little foam around the notes. The final divertissement, or *Feria*, had perhaps some influence on Debussy's *Ibéria*, which was composed very shortly afterwards; *Valence*, the third port of call in Jacques Ibert's *Escales*, was to recall both *Ibéria* and the *Feria*. This *Feria* uses five popular tunes: A, which is a prelude; B, lively, broken by the rattling of castanets; C, which seems to have escaped from one of Albeniz' collections; D, very Catalan too, with something of a fairground air, shouting out its refrain first below C, then above it; E, which sounds as though a barrel organ was grinding it out, until it shrieks stridently high up beyond a changed version of D. A big tutti, where one can distinguish B in C major and perfect chords, then A, shaking the orchestra until it leaps up with all its cymbals. A tonadilla, as in the *Malagueña*, comes to interrupt the joyful frenzy of this dance; this intermezzo,[1] a slow waltz in F sharp, has a most expressive melody which descends through various stresses, portandos, repeated notes and two successive modulations until it reaches its lower tonic. A few remnants of the opening serenade then reappear, influenced by the thirds in C, and then embroidered onto the B theme. Chords with passionate modifications in the style of the *Trio* open the final *stretto* for which the nocturne,

with its four nostalgic notes carved out into feverish triplets of quavers forms first the bass, then superimposes in capricious counterpoints fragments borrowed from all the themes of the *Rhapsodie*. This shattering Feria, where fury and exaltation themselves obey the dictates of the mind, has the verve of Chabrier, but it is possible to recognise in certain modulations and discords at the end a tragic element which looks forward to *La Valse*.

Daphnis et Chloé (1911), which aims at being a 'choreographic

[1] Cf. the Finale of the violin Sonata by Debussy, p. 18-19.

47

Costume for the chief of the brigands in 'Daphnis et Chloé' (Bakst).

symphony' is built up on five essential themes: A, spread out over a scaffolding of six fifths, serves as a kind of frontispiece and causes an obstinately discordant D sharp to resound over the A, the tonic bass; during this time the choirs behind the scene sing B, which represents the call of nature. C, the love theme of Daphnis, stands out almost at once against the same vocal background. The Chloé theme, (D), the fourth of the symphony, appears later[1] in the form of a graceful waltz. E, a trumpet call, which can be considered as the theme of the pirates, is stated towards the end of the first part. In spite of this rigid thematic plan and the unity of the key of A major, *Daphnis* is well composed as a ballet, that is to say like a suite of dances linked by the thread of a conventional argument: a sacred dance, which is rather stiff, and with its repeats, its great arpeggios, its slow tempo, resembles all sacred dances and all school cantatas; dances for the young girls, then for the young men, which are

[1]   P. 22 of the piano edition (theme E appears p. 35).

48

Costumes for 'Daphnis and Chloé' (Bakst).

then 'married' together by the most graceful of counterpoints; a grotesque dance for Dorcon the cowman, the contrasting graceful dance for Daphnis, in the form of a barcarolle; this competition ends with the apotheosis of C, which, blazing with the fire of its seven sharps, shines gloriously, as in duets from opera, through the golden cloud of the choirs singing with their mouths closed. A shortened re-exposition[1] of the prelude, a free cadence for the clarinet, a fleeting reminiscence of Daphnis' dance, and in the depths the expiring C theme, all announce Lyceion, the Salome of Greece, and her dance with the veils; it is impossible to remain untouched by these major sevenths, this tender voice, coming no doubt from the Quartet, that we have already heard twice, in *L'Indifférent* from *Shéhérazade* and in the intermezzo from *Laideronnette*.

---

[1] P. 31; for these rising fourths and fifths in triplets of quavers, cf. p. 3. These two pages are very much like Debussy.

Wonderful tremolos, above which A can be heard in a strongly discordant juxtaposition, follow the capture of Chloé by the pirates and precede the strange groupings, the insolent basses of the dance of the nymphs. The first part of the ballet ends with a rather tortuous a capella chorus with B in syncopation forming the foreground, while two trumpets behind the scenes sound the B theme. The second tableau, which represents the pirates' camp, opens with a scene reminiscent of *Gwendoline*, while it would not be too difficult, either, to track down a memory of Borodin; in the barbarous march which dominates, as by right, the F theme, we can hear the shouts of the Vikings and the Polovtsi passing by. In contrast to these warlike sounds – savage cries, the rattle of arms, subdued footsteps, the beat of horses' hooves – the third tableau begins full of darkness and silence; only the liquid murmur of little streams which laugh softly among the rocks; then, with the first white streaks of dawn, while the birds begin their chorus and the notes of a shepherd's flute, as in Debussy, reach the rim of the horizon with the light wind of morning, a wonderful melody, sustained by B behind the scenes, rises from the depths of all nature and mounts irresistibly towards a climax, after the two themes of Chloé and Daphnis have finally come together.[1] The commentary of the shepherd Lammon, which forms one of Ravel's most refined pages, precedes the parable of Pan and Syrinx; and just as Roussel was to recount the birth of the lyre, so Ravel sings the birth of the flute, in F sharp, to a habanera rhythm with the bass sustaining a great nostalgic *Vocalise* for the instrument; huge chords with appoggiaturas which sound as though they are going to be resolved into G major, continually come up against the ostinato tonic and dominant. The A theme, reappearing in its original key in the midst of the grandiose calls of B signifying the oath of Daphnis, forms a prelude to the final bacchanale; this last dance, with its dionysiac glow, gleams momentarily with steely flashes which recall *La Péri* or *The Firebird*, ends like the other Feria, the Spanish Feria, in the disciplined jubilation of every kind of rhythm.

Ravel's music only entered the theatre on two occasions, and the first time with *L'Heure espagnole* in 1907. Three essential motives share the conduct of music which, in spite of appearing to go through a re-exposition,[2] comes near to reaching

---

[1]   Compare p. 80 and the first movement of the Trio.

[2]   P. 72 of the piano and vocal score.

L'heure Espagnole

L'Heure espagnole, le brillant petit acte de M. Franc-Nohain, pour lequel M. Maurice Ravel écrivit une partition du plus curieux inédit, vaut se prévaloir justement d'une interprétation hors de pair. En effet, Mlle Vix, étrange et troublant Zulinga, a apporté dans la composition du rôle de Conception l'originalité précieuse qui la classe parmi les meilleures cantatrices lyriques de notre époque. M. Jean Périer, dont le talent souligne si plaisamment la critique, fait pour l'admirable chanteur et l'admirable acteur qu'on connaît, et MM. De-Voye, Coulomb et Cazeneuve contribuèrent certes, pour beaucoup, à la réussite de cet ouvrage très applaudi. Au milieu de la page : M. PÉRIER, à gauche en haut : M. PÉRIER, en bas : Mlle VIX, à droite en haut : M. COULOMB, en bas : M. DELVOYE.

the extreme limit of breakdown and discontinuity: the first theme, opening on an E bass, and proceeding sometimes at the cost of harsh discords, in parallel six-four chords, is nothing more than the clock theme; with its trimming of carillons, timbres and chimes, it expresses, as Roland-Manuel said, 'the soul of the enchanted shop'. The second theme, which sounds very athletic, characterises Ramiro the muleteer; the theme may become scattered, may pass into triple time like a waltz, or slow down over a bass in the tonic,[1] but it can never lose its sporting air and its muscular rhythms. The third theme, introduced by four horns, is a kind of heroic march which emphasises every appearance of Don Iñigo, the fat lover. Iñigo is a reincarnation of the Peacock in the *Histoires naturelles*. The conclusion, with its dazzling vocal quintet, worthy of the burlesque finale of *La Farce du Cuvier*, by Gabriel Dupont, follows naturally from the melodious mist of the prelude; it consists of a habanera in G major comprising three tunes, the third very popular in style, the second in B minor marking the rhythms of the rapid *vocalises* sung by the actors who stand in a row facing the public. The clocks and the grotesque Iñigo Gomez of *L'Heure espagnole* come to life again in the villain and the Corregidor of *Le Tricorne*.[2] Certainly there is more popular vitality in de Falla, and more subtle refinement in Ravel, more poetry in the Andalusian, more humour and acid cheerfulness in the Frenchman; but the fact is that the farce adapted from Alarcon supplies the argument for a ballet for which the choreography imposes natural repetitions, while Franc-Nohain's vaudeville, with its caustic licentiousness, is at the origin of a musical comedy perpetually broken up by dialogue; *Le Tricorne* is danced and mimed, whereas *L'Heure espagnole* is sung. This is why it was Ravel who showed the way to Manuel de Falla.

[1] P. 48-49 (*A* pedal) and 70-71 (*F* pedal).
[2] Compare *El Sombrero* p. 11 (piano solo) and the little waltz of *L'Heure espagnole*, p. 88. Also: *El Sombrero*, p. 24-25 (descending scale of harmonies of fourth and sixth parallels) and *L'Heure espagnole* p. 88, 91 (p. and ch.)

*With Hélène Jourdan-Morhange and Ricardo Viñes
on the beach at Saint-Jean-de-Luz (1923).*

III. 1918-1937

The years just after the war, like those just before, do not show any continuous line of development in Ravel's work. His writing was becoming continually harder and more aggressive now, but the three songs entitled *Don Quichotte à Dulcinée*, the *Boléro* and the Concertos (especially the Concerto for Left Hand) represent in some way a return to indulgence. Thus it happened that at the end of a scrupulous life lived under progressively greater strain by his refusal to make any concessions, the artist lingered a few moments in the oasis of pleasure. These were the harmonies of twilight. During the increasingly severe discipline that Fauré imposed on himself at the end of his life the Twelfth Barcarolle in E flat minor and the Fourth Prelude in F represent in the same way moments of delightful abandonment. Even the cruel Debussy of the *Epigraphes* and the *Douze Etudes* period allowed himself from time to time to be mellowed by sweet memories of youth. He was very human,

53

perhaps too human. Even more than Fauré, Ravel experienced those delightful defeats of will power. And yet it cannot be denied that in their entirety the works written after 1918, including the bright Concerto in G Major, which are all so airy and limpid, express in their way the return to simplicity preached by the later Bergson. At this point Ravel reacted not only against the complications of style of the d'Indy school, which he already repudiated in the *Sonatine*, the *Chanson limousine* and the *Petit Poucet*, but against his own harmonic subtleties. First he renounced the powerful basses of *Les Grands vents Venus d'outremer*: the melody of the violin sonata and the Ronsard *Epitaphe* float through the air without the deep support of an accompaniment well implanted in the bass. In this respect too *Laideronnette* may be said to have shown the way; but all that was achieved in *Ma Mère l'oye* through skilful simplicity now becomes the composer's normal style. The rich tonalities – the F sharp major of *Manteau de fleurs* and *Laideronnette*, the C sharp major of *Ondine*, give way to more ascetic keys: E minor most of all, the blue-toned E of Fauré's last works, as in *Le Tombeau de Couperin*, and its relative G major (*L'Enfant et les sortilèges*, Concerto, the violin Sonata, *Berceuse* on the name of Faure, *Chanson à boire*, and the minuet from *Le Tombeau de Couperin*), as well as the combination A minor C major (Duo for violin and cello), already present in the *Pavane* and *Le Jardin féerique* which form the framework for *Ma Mère l'oye*. Instead of the clay that is pliable, coloured and already melodious, on which one can make an impression without meeting resistance, Ravel now prefers hard, cold steel. He goes further; Ravel heroically represses within himself this taste for full, rich sonority, so vibrant and truly instrumental, which is so obvious in the finale to the *Trio* or in the *Rhapsodie espagnole*; this can be seen in *L'Enfant et les sortilèges* and the air for the Princess, a perfectly unadorned arabesque, in counterpoint to a melody for the flute; the two voices, as in *Rêves* or in the Fugue from *Le Tombeau de Couperin*, move between heaven and earth; during the course of this airy badinage the lower melodic line sometimes rises higher than the other, and this produces knottiness, acid unison and harsh friction; from this comes all the hardness of the *Sonate en Duo*, all the humble linearity of *Nahandove* and the third *Chanson madécasse*. One might say that the taste for horizontal monody, for writing as fine as a thread and counterpoint in two parts, with Ravel as

54

with Satie, corresponds to the 'return to drawing' that Cocteau advocated after the war and that Guillaume Apollinaire, on his side, greeted with delight in Matisse. The *Trois beaux oiseaux du Paradis* and also *Nicolette*, in which the thread had gradually shrunk until it was no more than a point, a tonic note, already prepared the way for this narrowing down of the melody; also, in the *Passacaille* from the Trio, and the *Berceuse sur le nom de Fauré* in which the staves empty themselves of the groups of notes and the complex chords previously adorning them, the melody became more bare and gradually achieved again the linear austerity of the beginning; the harmonies, in the Russian manner, often combined with the unison again. There is a very solemn moment in *Ondine* when the symphony of countless arpeggios and springs of water has died away and the voice of the fairy emerges, totally alone and totally fragile in the midst of silence. It is the same voice that rises at dawn at the opening of the third part of *Daphnis et Chloé*, mingling with the songs of the birds and the murmur of the streams. The Ravel of the last years, with his search for economy, perpetuated this Ondine voice, this recitative of the soul, this solo sung in the midst of silence.

The same simplification of diction and the same resistance to harmonic inflation characterise also the evolution of Fauré. But while Fauré never renounced the soft velvet of the low notes he seems, as he became simpler, to pursue a dream completely within his own mind. Ravel, who was more nervous and more aggressive, toyed with scandal and harsh friction; the provocation of bitonality was a kind of wager for him. It is true that Ravel underwent influences which passed by Fauré without even touching him; since he was younger, Ravel was also more closely mingled in the post war fever – eroticism, sport, neurasthenia, the worship of machines, which at no moment had ever troubled the Olympic serenity of Fauré; and it is strange that this dizzy modernity, which carved out all the whirlwinds of *La Valse chorégraphique*, brought so few wrinkles to the face of the Quartet in 1924. Later, Ravel was attracted by the abstract researches of Schoenberg, and the *Trois Poèmes de Mallarmé* prove that this curiosity dates from before the 1914 war; perhaps it was this that caused Ravel's growing taste for small instrumental ensembles, to which we owe the *Trois poèmes* and the *Chansons madécasses*, but also Stravinsky's *Berceuses du chat* and the *Pribaoutki*, and even *L'Histoire du soldat*. From the time of the first Valse Noble there is a tendency for the basses to climb by intervals of a fourth, a tendency more and more clearly visible in the third *Chanson madécasse*, and especially in the Andante of the *Sonate en Duo*, where at the end the tonality sinks right down. Ravel had too pleasure-loving an ear and too much hostility to systems to enclose himself definitely within any prejudice in favour of austerity and anti-hedonism. The insatiable curiosity of a gourmet anxious to try everything had brought him closer, as early as 1913, to *Pierrot lunaire*, with the result that polytonality itself was for him an untried and particularly subtle form of pleasure. In fact Schoenberg interested him as much as Gershwin; for this same hunger for novelty took him also to the music hall and to jazz; he certainly revelled in American Negro music, as can be seen from the fox-trots and boston two-steps of *L'Enfant et les sortilèges*, the duple rhythms worthy of the Weill of *Mahagonny*, and the nostalgic blues which serves as andante to the Sonata for piano and violin. The Finale to Debussy's Sonata in G minor had undergone this attractive influence, without which Satie's *Parade*, Milhaud's *Rag-Caprices*, and Stravinsky's *Rag-time* and *Piano Rag-music* would not exist.

During these post-war years Ravel's piano work consisted only of *Le Tombeau de Couperin* (1917) and the two Concertos (1932). *Le Tombeau*, composed in the form of a suite, opens with a delightful Prelude full of whirling triplets. The Fugue consists of delicate badinage with a subject appearing in E in the right hand, then in the left hand in B, a fourth below, then in counterpoint against a counter-subject recognisable by its triplet of quavers. The two voices oppose each other, converse, turn round, go down once to the bass, and then, after various antics, the pleasant dialogue dies away in the centre of the keyboard. The melancholy and noble Forlane, with its discordant modulations, resembles a cradle-song with undulations which join together three inter-mezzi, finishing with a most severe coda. The C major of the Rigaudon is very square and resonant, forming a most pleasant contrast with this faded nobility; it is worth noting the swift cadences which unexpectedly resolve into C at the moment when it seemed that the dance was going to end in G or F; the rustic grace of the intermezzo which here takes the place of a trio interrupts the Rigaudon for a moment. The graceful Minuet becomes enthusiastic in its 'musette' until it reaches an almost pathetic fortissimo, then in the most charming way adds below the theme of the Minuet the perfect chords of a musette that has gone into the major; finally the Minuet divides into two on its way to a very sedate coda that is not unrelated to the grace of the earlier Debussy. The misty trill on which the dance ends is a counterpart to the long final tremolo of the Prelude which was in a sense the final whirling of the triplets which had been brought to a standstill: the triplets throb and vibrate without moving like the blades of a diapason.[1] The rustling *Toccata* reproduces a certain number of the technical difficulties of *Scarbo* – repeated notes, alternating thirds, the intimate collaboration of the two hands; the pianism is highly emphasised, startling and limpid, less imaginative perhaps than that of *Scarbo*.

The two Concertos,[2] although contemporary (1931), are very different in character, and yet the Concerto in G, in spite of appearances, is not more Ravelian than the Concerto in D; the truth is that the latter, through the paradoxical limitations that it imposes, was intended to give more value to a demonstration of power, and this is the reason for its decorative, almost grandiose character, which is different in every way from the exuberant jubilation of the Concerto in G. The Concerto in D, although one can easily distinguish andante, scherzo and finale, is played without interruption in one single movement made up of movements linked together. It begins in the deep notes of the orchestra, with a confused jumble of fourths in sextuplets above which a kind of majestic March slowly rises, like the Waltz in the poem of 1919. The Concerto for two hands, on the contrary, begins directly in the upper regions, the most limpid and luminous part of the keyboard and the orchestra; for here the piano is in concert from the first bar; instead of mysterious basses and the fumblings of improvisation we can hear, through the bitonal piano arpeggios, a kind of cheerful and almost popular song. In the Concerto in D the solo left hand, after a thunderous start, solemnly plays the triumphal March from the prelude (the saraband, says Goldbeck) and lines up a set of chords which compose a gateway to the Concerto, a kind of monumental colonnade; the orchestra, playing tutti, takes up again this paean issuing from an irresistible inspiration. The Andante, compressed and reduced to an intermezzo in an unbroken symphony, does not succeed in expressing itself as broadly as the Andante in E major from the other Concerto: here the piano sings an admirable *lied*, a long, serene

---

[1] Cf. Ernesto Halffter, *Sonatina*, p. 38 (piano solo).
[2] See Fr. Goldbeck's study, *Sur Ravel et ses Concertos*, *Revue musicale*, 1933, p. 193-200.

effusion that the orchestra takes up later, with a pianissimo accompaniment of demisemiquavers which run up and down on the keyboard like warm, even and tranquil rain. The Concerto in G, which has only three movements, all of them very different in character, ends with a metallic Rondo, while the Concerto in D includes further a kind of choreographic scherzo with sighing rag-time sounds, an obsessive bass and many rhythmic *divertissements*. Sometimes it is all slightly exterior, but it rings clear and hard.

The vocal compositions in the post-war period include *Ronsard à son âme*, a true epigraph in the old style, (1924) and, based on words by Fargue, *Rêves*, which is reminiscent of Laforgue's Sundays and Claude Monet's *Gare Saint-Lazare*, a rather disturbing melody with its sedate air and then, at the end, the harsh bitonal C sharp of its basses. But most of all the *Chansons madécasses*, created by Madeleine Grey in 1925, are the characteristic work of the post-war period, just as the *Histoires naturelles* dominated the production of the impressionist period. The instrumental ensemble is even more ascetic than that of the Mallarmé *Poèmes* since there is only one flute instead of two, no clarinets at all and one cello for all four strings. This cycle is truly a collection of exemplary simplicity – the voice hardly sings at all, and sometimes the recitative seems strangely indifferent to the words that are being declaimed; moreover the apparent

The inhabitants of Madagascar (XVIIIth century drawing).

Lithograph by Luc-Albert Moreau for 'Les Chansons madécasses'.

independence of the superimposed lines does not exclude the exact adjustment of the voice to the rhythms of the accompaniment.[1] In *Nahandove*, a love nocturne, we notice first a cradle-song rhythm with a fourth and an obsessive seventh that seems to haunt all the last works of Ravel[2] – *Rêves*, *L'Enfant et les sortilèges*, where these intervals are sometimes tense, sometimes naïve, and the violin Sonata:

Rêves   *Nahandove*   *Sonate*   *L'Enfant et les Sortilèges*

then come breathless rhythms, punctuated with hard sounds; and then again the modest cradle-song, barely affected by the languors of the text. The second poém, *Aoua*, is only a cry – a hoarse, wild, discordant cry which is sometimes reminiscent of the heart-rending

[1] P. 4-5 of the piano and vocal edition, note the crowded fifths as in Ronsard's *Epitaphe*.
[2] *Chansons madécasses*, piano and vocal edition, p. 6 (and 14); *Rêves*, *L'Enfant et les sortilèges*, p. 25 and 93-97; violin Sonata, p. 3, 6, 9 (and 22) and the songs of the nightingale and the owl in *L'Enfant et les sortilèges*, p.64.

59

calls of *Pierrot Lunaire*; everything here is misery – the cruel bitonal atmosphere, the menacing rhythms, and the basses which are taunted by a mortal anguish. After these cries the third song unfolds a slender melody on the flute which proceeds very freely by intervals of a fourth and ends as a calm nocturne in D flat major; after the noise of war come the peaceful siesta, the great peace of evening and the humble occupations of everyday. In this way the midday rest which ends at twilight meets the southern nocturne of the beginning and closes admirably the triptych of the *Chansons madécasses*. In contrast to the refinement of this last group the three songs *Don Quichotte à Dulcinée* (1934), written to somewhat pretentious words, are more popular in accent and certainly of a much flimsier fabric; in the *Chanson romantique* and the *Chanson à boire* we can hear again without displeasure the ritournelle of Gonzalve, the amorous fool of *L'Heure espagnole*: 'Harpes, chantez, éclatez, salves!'... But the streaming appoggiaturas of 1907 have disappeared. The *Chanson épique*, which is a little stiff, affects the appearance of a hymn. The pleasant *Chanson à boire*, with its concerted vulgarity, evokes simultaneously both Chabrier and the Tenth Spanish Dance by Granados; with its ritournelle of alternating perfect chords, its grace-notes like those already used in the *Boléro*,[1] its good-natured modulation into C major and the symmetry of its stanzas, this drinking song shows a complete break with the harmonic affectation of *Placet futile*.

Ravel's last instrumental work includes two sonatas which indicate an essential step in his development. But first we should mention a few works of lesser importance: first, a subtle *Berceuse* on the name of Fauré (1922), which is only a 'berceuse' in fact because of a subsidiary theme played in general in the upper register by the violin while the left hand picks out the twelve

---

[1] Cf. Turina, *Tres Arias*, III (*Rima*).

letters of Gabriel Fauré's name in C or G and the right hand plays bitonal chords or discordant major sevenths; at the end the piano, with no bass, and accompanied on the violin by simple oscillating seconds, plays the chosen theme with a kind of childlike innocence, and the *berceuse* dies away on gently resonant wrong notes – F sharp or E flat vibrating over the tonic G. *Tzigane* (1924) was originally written as a rhapsody for violin and *luthéal* and like a good rhapsody it sounds like a string of successive variations juxtaposed without development. After a great concert preamble (Lassan) in which the violin openly surrenders itself to various superior exercises – runs, staccato notes, trills and mordents, a thu crous cadence on the *luthéal* inaugurates the traditional series of gipsy improvisations – the Friska, then the Czardas. The recitative of the solo violin plays alternately a slow, solemn and pompous theme, with a strong gipsy flavour, and another which is more expressive and more danceable, which re-establishes itself in B flat minor. This recitative which includes notes of very unequal value, going from the minim to the demisemiquaver, is interrupted by the inevitable Rubato, a more affectionate phrase which, however, soon becomes excitable and degenerates into hectic *vocalises*. At the end the rhapsody becomes impatient and runs feverishly through all kinds of successive tonalities without retaining any of them; the gypsy ornaments – turns of short notes, strident trills on minor seconds – and also the hard discords compose for this *stretto* the most dazzling ornamentation imaginable. The Duo in the form of a Sonata for violin and 'cello is perhaps the most outstanding of Ravel's successes. In the first movement four principal motifs can be distinguished: A, an arpeggio played by the violin, is repeated eight times like the theme of a cradle song and becomes fairly quickly a simple orna-ment or decorative accompaniment. On this theme the cello develops in A, (then the violin in D, a fourth higher), and from the sixth bar a counter-theme B appears, with a false innocence not unlike *Ma Mère l'oye*. The third theme appears in equal crotchets on the violin (C) and the fourth, in B minor (D), is similar to those old French rounds which make their cheerful bright appearance in the work of Poulenc. Several subordinate themes proceed from B. D, for example, which is completely atonal. The counterpoints between the two instruments are continually reversed while, as they are repeated, the four themes seem to trace dance figures. The Scherzo, a kind of aggressive game like the Pantoum in the Trio and the intermezzo from the

Concerto for the Left Hand, but more stark and acid, sets out a first theme A which is no more than the sketch for A, played in pizzicato crotchets on the two instruments alternately; B, like D, resembles a popular round. Just as the Passacaglia in the *Trio* rose from the bass notes of the keyboard, so the Adagio from the Sonata rises from the depths of the cello which passes over to the violin again an orison entirely collected from the austere greyness of A minor; the atonal motif of the first movement reappears next with its intractable major seventh movements.[1] Finally the Adagio sets out again its melody over melancholy cello percussion and the meditation ends in the mystery of the basses moving in fourths. The Finale introduces three new themes, not counting subsidiary motifs: A, played in energetic rhythm on the cello, rising gradually from one octave to another. B appears in syncopation, carried by a trill on the cello; and C, played in F sharp with the tip of the bow, on the cello, then accompanied by tremolos on a major seventh, is also a 'joyeuse marche'. The violin takes it up again in A, supported by the cello in tremolos of chromatically descending perfect chords, and finally adds it to A. Two old themes reappear in this Finale: firstly, A, its echoes going backwards and forwards in canon between the cello and the violin; next the atonal theme of the first movement, which the cello plays mischievously in syncopation to the second half of C. While the Sonata in A minor, with two violins, succeeded in creating an impression of luxuriant life and polyphonic richness, the Sonata in G major,[2] with a piano, achieves on the other hand the most perfect simplicity. It is dedicated to Hélène Jourdan-Morhange, who first performed it. To a long 6/8 – 9/8 rhythm the piano first plays A, a pastoral

---

[1] See the analysis of Florent Schmitt in *Le Temps* of the 22nd January 1938.
[2] Cf. the themes p. 189.

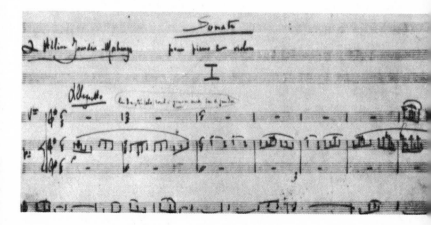

theme in G major taken up again by the violin a fifth higher above octaves struck on the piano; below repeated B flats in the right hand, the left hand then plays B, distinguished by its repeated staccato notes. Next come the austere fifths of the Ronsard *Epitaphe* and *L'Enfant et les sortilèges* (p. 84), supporting a third theme, C, which is very expressive. D, consisting of more serious perfect chords juxtaposed on the piano, and E, played by the violin for a long time after the re-exposition, complete the thematic scheme of this first movement, where we can hear again something of the supremely simple duet between the Child and the Fairy, evaporating finally in a graceful badinage deprived of any support from the bass. A nostalgic 'blues' serves as andante, and a 'Perpetuum mobile' as Finale. Poulenc humorously gave the title 'Mouvements perpétuels' to three short pieces which are neither perpetual nor particularly mobile. Ravel revives the very mobility of the romantic Presto and the virtuosity of Paganini: the repeated notes, the virtuoso passages and violin arpeggios play the same role in this Finale as the unbroken melody for the right hand in the Finale of Weber's first Sonata, or in Mendelssohn's Sonata in C major, opus 119. After a re-collection of the B theme which is linked with the final seventh of the Blues, the 'Perpetuum mobile' ends by recalling A, the pastoral theme, set out in crotchets and doubled in fifths; the last bars are not without a recollection of the peroration of the Quartet.

La Valse (1919) is, with the *Boléro*, the only purely symphonic work of the post-war period; even then it is not purely a symphonic poem in the Liszt tradition, but a ballet, and its choreographic argument replaces the long 'programmes' that Liszt the ideologist and metaphysician wrote at the head of his compositions. 1919, the very year of peace... How different is this music from the *Valses nobles et sentimentales* written in 1910 above the *mêlée* by a composer who believed himself frivolous. From the change of key we can guess the catastrophe that has overthrown the world and is to separate the old Europe from the new. The composer of *La Valse* is no longer a dilettante in search of 'useless occupations'... Here there is no suite of dances, as in *Adélaïde*, but one waltz only, a great and tragic waltz which is entirely on its own and both noble and sentimental all at once, but this time seriously so. No more rigaudons, mischievous pranks and rustic picnics. It is not that *La Valse* does not often quote from the eight waltzes of 1910, especially the seventh; we have already encountered their fortissimos. No matter: there is an element of anguish in this tremendous crescendo cut in two by a re-exposition. The dance tune emerges from the mist at the eleventh bar, becomes gradually more and more passionate until it reaches its climax, then, rejecting one by one all the keys that it approaches, passes, towards the end, through moments of impatience and hardness which recall, with increased ferocity, the breathless peroration of the *Alborada* or *Daphnis et Chloé* and look forward to the final enervation of *Tzigane*.[1]

For the second and last time, in 1925, Ravel's music went on to the stage; *L'Enfant et les sortilèges* (1920–1925) adopted in its turn this numbered plan which is so dear to the choreographer and represents practically what would have been the episodic argument in *Shéhérazade*, where the successive tales of the Sultana follow each other: the succession of the enchantments corresponds here to the dreams of Florine in *Ma Mère l'oye*, the flower allegories in *Adélaïde*, the dances in *Daphnis et Chloé* and even the misunderstandings of *L'Heure espagnole*. There are no themes, unless the two tender chords signifying 'maman'[2] can be called such; at the start they change key through the child's naughtiness, and reappear at the end, first of all timid, then solemn, like a message from all nature, affectionate and resonant finally like goodness itself. And yet Ravel's writing had never been so mischievous: the chords representing the Franche-Comté clock that has gone wrong, the shouts of Father Arithmetic and the pointed sarcasms which laugh over every octave fill this score with their stridency.[3] The language of *Adélaïde* lives again in these pages, notably in the scene with the tomcats where the lingering chords carry a surprising and straightforward echo of the fifth waltz, the slow waltz and the sixth, both of them mingled together in the eighth.[4] But it is more *Ma Mère l'oye* that comes to life again in this melancholy pastoral in A where a D bass. the subdominant, marks out the alternating rhythm of a choir of shepherd lads

---

[1] Compare: piano edition, p. 22 and a cadenza of the Concerto in G, first movement, p. 14.

[2] Change of key p. 3-4; timid call: p. 86; solemn: p. 97-98; smooth: p. 101.

[3] Note however p. 13 a perfect chord of E flat minor with rising arpeggio and descending scale. In this way Debussy in *Pelléas* arranges concordant calm passages which are in a sense the oases of diatonism.

[4] *L'Enfant et les sortilèges*, p. 61-63 and 86; *Valses nobles et sentimentales*, p. 24.

Father Arithmetic's costume for 'L'Enfant et les sortilèges' (P. Colin).

and lasses. The result is a set of exquisite sevenths. The very American Waltz of the dragonflies prepares the way for the elevenths of the Concerto for the Left Hand.[1] And so that love may have the last word, it is worth listening carefully to this final chorus in G major where, behind the fifths of the prelude, played now more slowly (crotchets replacing quavers) there sings the voice of a tender heart. But who should one listen to, the artisan or the poet? the engineer of so many precision machines or the passionate lyric writer? Between the sarcasms of Father Arithmetic and the sweet melody, the maternal theme and Fire, the industrious soldier, the blacksmith with his scarlet tongues and thousand sparks, it is not easy to take a decision.

---

[1] *L'Enfant et les sortilèges*, p. 69-71 and 85; and compare Concerto for the Left Hand, (p. 9).

Skill

'Ah! I can see clearly into my heart.'
(Marivaux)

The music of Ravel proves that France is the country not of moderation but of passionate extremism and acute paradox. It is a question of testing out how far the mind can go in any given direction, of taking without any weakening all the possible consequences of certain attitudes. The result is adventure, scandal and the abandonment of prejudices; we are led to this point by the passionate, bold French imagination, which is not afraid of going to the extreme limits of its power. There is no question of attributing to Ravel a mediocre mind occupied with outstripping others or breaking records for their own sake. Further, music, as Louis Laloy[1] so reasonably believed, is not a science capable of making indefinite progress through the discovery of new chords, or the gradual enrichment and complication of harmony. It would be wrong therefore to believe that Ravel went further than Debussy in an 'armaments race' in which Stravinsky in his turn would have gone further still; this strictly linear and quantitative view of progress, if it is true of technicalities, gives the lie to the revolutionary vocation of art. And yet it cannot be denied that Ravel obeyed a kind of law of frenzy, normal to every kind of passionate geometry. There is no ground therefore for making invidious comparisons between the one-directional development of Ravel and the many-sided, unforeseeable evolution of Roussel: the alliance of logic and passion is one of the most noticeable characteristics of the 18th century and it is not surprising that Ravel was constantly attracted by a

---

[1] Louis Laloy, *La Musique retrouvée*, p. 166-167. Roland-Manuel, *Maurice Ravel et son œuvre dramatique*, p. 87.

The study at Montfort.

period which was at the same time the century of great ideological audacity and of the most exquisite refinements of manners, luxury and voluptuousness.

The pseudo Monticelli of which Ravel was so proud . . .

Challenge

Ravel's audacity expresses itself in two ways – firstly in a liking for difficulties overcome and an obstinate search for effort, and secondly in the spirit of artifice. Roland-Manuel, who penetrated more deeply than anyone else into the secrets of Ravel's art spoke of the 'aesthetics of imposture'. It seems preferable to say 'aesthetics of challenge', for a challenge implies a *tour de force* and an iron will. This side of the challenge is both Cornelian and Stoic. Having found that beautiful things are difficult, Ravel then played at creating artificially the exceptional, thankless and paradoxical conditions which re-establish the hardness that is beauty; since he did not experience the romantic conflict between vocation and destiny,[1] he invented, for he had no natural difficulty in expressing himself,

[1] Ravel, p. 199-200. *Revue musicale*, number quoted, p. 16.

artificial obstacles which caused him a second type of clumsiness;
he fabricated for his own use gratuitous prohibitions and arbitrary
orders, voluntarily impoverished his own language, and tried
all types of limitations, distortion and stridency in order to
prove with certainty how much an artist's effort can achieve.
The poet compels himself to write in verse and the musician
accepts the rules of the fugue; for this narrowness, which lies
at the origin of duty, is above all the way of the poet just as
it is the way of the virtuoso. Alain was fond of discovering
this in Victor Hugo:[1] *Les Djinns* for instance is a kind of calli-
gram and a successful bet. Ravel would have liked not only
the conventional rules and the veto, the word-puzzles and the
riddles, but the artificial dangers as well; for will-power is stronger
than death – either I will overcome this difficulty before the
tenth stroke of ten o'clock – some deserving, fantastic and
disinterested act – or I will blow my brains out. Every composition by Ravel represents in this sense a certain problem
to be solved, a game in which the player voluntarily makes
the rules of the game more complicated; although nobody
makes him do so he places restrictions on himself and learns,
as Nietzsche would have said, 'to dance in chains'... This
is both strength and weakness, richness and poverty. Some
aspects of this poverty, through energy and tour de force, become
more opulent than opulence: first, melodic poverty, as in the
Boléro which fixes us with its glittering eyes and fascinates us;
the *Boléro*, which M. Dumesnil compares to a perpetual *Da
capo*, has sworn that it will fill half an hour of music with a
theme lasting for sixteen bars and including no development
or variation, by the mere diversity of its instrumentation, that
is to say by the adjunction of new timbres – flute, clarinet, oboe,
trombone and saxophone – which is made rhythmic by the
unceasing obsessive percussion of the side-drum; the instrumental colour makes the uniformity tolerable, as in Rimsky-
Korsakov's *Capriccio espagnol*, and demonstrates triumphantly
what can be called the variety of monotony. This is very simple,
but somebody had to think of it first. Second, harmonic
poverty: *Ronsard à son âme*, which is written entirely in
one stave, undertakes to employ, from start to finish, only
open fifths: icy, hard fifths, not at all like the thirds of the

---

[1] *Préliminaires à l'Esthétique*, propos 93-94. Nietzsche, *Der Wanderer und
sein Schatten* II, 140 and 159. Cf. 170. The poet as 'imposter': I, 32. Cf.
II, 122.

Inscription sur le sable, but bare, cold and smooth like the marble on tombstones. The succession of fifths seems to build up at the end in order to support the last chord, consisting of seven fifths piled on top of each other, from the fundamental A to the top A sharp, as happens below the A theme in *Daphnis*. The prelude to *L'Enfant et les sortilèges*, with its parallel fourths and fifths juxtaposed in the upper register on two oboes achieves an exploit of the same kind. Third, polyphonic poverty, as in the *Sonate en Duo* for violin and cello, tortuous *badinage* in which two voices in counterpoint pursue each other, catch each other and lose each other again, without the support of any accompaniment; here Ravel undertakes to 'shape a whole symphony using only his thumb and first finger',[1] and he compensates for the rarity of the notes and the poverty of the chords by the mercurial mobility of two parts which manage to be everywhere at the same time. In the opposite way to the *Epitaphe*, written for the right hand only, the Concerto for the Left Hand is an exercise almost as successful, written in the heroic tradition of Liszt, Liapounov and Scriabin: Ladies and gentlemen, you are going to witness everything that one man can do with the five fingers of his left hand. And in fact, just as Liszt, through ingenious economy, the crossing of hands and the alternation of chords, endowed the sonority of the piano with orchestral volume, so Ravel obtains more with five fingers than others do with all the voices of the orchestra. In the same way Bartok wrote a transcendant Sonata for solo violin. And another ascetism of a new type: Ravel cheerfully chose flat or antipoetic words – Jules Renard's prose, Parny's narrative style, Franc-Nohain's rhymes, Verlaine's disjointed phrases in *Sur l'herbe* – for he purposely chose the driest scene from *Fêtes galantes*.[2] The most praiseworthy poetry is surely that which is wrung from the hardest material. This is what makes the *Histoires naturelles* into such a paradoxical success, and one wonders still how he was able to extract such a rare emotion from the humble words that end the third *Chanson madécasse*: 'Go, and prepare the meal...' The soloist recites these words 'quasi parlando' and everything is as simple as a still life by Cézanne – a poor bowl on a poor table – only the poor things of every day. One is reminded of the fantastic idea

[1]   E. Vuillermoz, *Musiques d'aujourd'hui*, p. 160.
[2]   Léon Guichard, *Le Point*, Septembre 1938, p. 191.

of Satie who, as a challenge, set the *Phaedo* to music and used the prosaic prose translation of Victor Cousin. Many other problems have been solved by Ravel: the *Valse chorégraphique* which is, like the *Boléro*, the study of a crescendo; like the exordium of the Concerto in D it studies the progressive birth of a melody emerging gradually from confusion, which at the start, like the Passacaglia from the *Trio*, is a study on the low notes – *La Valse* wins almost every bet. Above all there is a form of poverty where this spirit of obsession and enchantment can be studied better still – the fascination with immobility that bewitches Stravinsky's 'Augures printaniers' and Falla's *El Amor Brujo* and which we find again in Ravel, in the reiteration of the *Boléro*, in the first movement of the *Sonate en Duo*, or the Scherzo from the Concerto in D, with its obstinate basses: the obsession with pedal notes – tonic or preferably dominant – perhaps remained with Ravel because of his study of Borodin; but Chopin's *Berceuse* op. 57 had already obstinately held a tonic pedal (D flat) for seventy-one bars, with the intention of hypnotising us. The astonishing *Gibet* in *Gaspard de la nuit* beats all the records, having vowed to hold a B flat pedal for fifty-two bars; and in fact the bet is won, the pianist does not release the throbbing B flat for one moment. Ravel's pedal notes represent therefore the motionless axis acting as pivot for the harmonies: sometimes it remains fixed,[1] mingling with the obsession of the rhythm, as in the *Boléro* and the Pastorale from *L'Enfant et les sortilèges*, in the poetic *Clair de lune*, op. 33 by Joseph Jongen, where the dominant F sharp hangs in the air as indolently as a dream; sometimes the pedal note flies from octave to octave;[2] sometimes it moves in order to bar the way to the huge chords with appoggiatura which are played by holding two notes down with the flat[3] of the thumb, while the pedal barrage prevents the chords from being resolved.

---

[1] *L'Heure espagnole*, p. 48-49 and 70-71; interlude of the *Noctuelles*; *Oiseaux tristes*; *Vallée des cloches*, passim; 8th *Valse noble*; *Kaddisch*, *Manteau de fleurs*; *L'Enfant et les sortilèges*, p. 31-40.

[2] Minuet from the *Tombeau de Couperin* (Musette), *Scarbo*, *Vocalise-étude*, *Chanson française*, *Placet futile*, *Trio* (1st Movement), Minuet from the *Sonatine*. Compare: Debussy, *Mouvement*. Cf. Fauré, 3rd *Valse-Caprice*.

[3] *Daphnis* (piano solo, p. 85-86), *Alborada* (*Miroirs*, p. 38, 40), *Barque sur l'océan* (*Miroirs*, p. 20), *Le Cygne*, *L'Heure espagnole* (piano and song, p. 108 and 19-21), *Habanera* from the *Rhapsodie espagnole*, 3rd *Valse noble* (p. 8-9), *La Valse* (piano solo, p. 10), *Asie* (*Shéhérazade*, p. 4 et 14), *Chanson de la mariée*. Cf. the interpolated recitatives from the *Danses du roi David* by Castelnuovo-Tedesco (imitating the sounds of the 'shofar').

Since the pedal remains as rigid as an iron bar while the harmonies change, the result is an insidious friction which Ravel exploits with skill, for he never tires of these clashing pedal notes. Perhaps Ravel was obsessed with pedal-notes, which attached him to a preoccupation with the dominant, or perhaps this mania was due quite simply to the influence of percussion instruments, such as tambourines[1] which produce only one unchanging note, whatever the turns and twists in the melodic line. It is possible to interpret it rather as the avariciously heroic method of a sensitivity which through practice has become economical in its own expression. Those hypnotic compositions, like Satie's first *Gnossienne*, Ravel's *Boléro* or *Le Gibet*, oppose 'Gnossian time', the Gorgon's head that immobilises sounds, to the spirit of mobility that circulates like quicksilver through the *Sonate en Duo* and *Scarbo*. It is in this respect that Ravel's music was from time to time incantatory like the stationary music of our time, like *Le Sacre du Printemps*, Villa-Lobos's *Cirandas*, Mompou's *Charmes*, de Falla's *Fantaisie bétique* and *Retable*. *L'Enfant et les sortilèges*, like *El Amor Brujo* reveals a preoccupation with the thrills and fascination of sorcery.

Artifice

Along with his fondness for challenge, 'artificiality' is Ravel's most striking characteristic. For Ravel, as for all true artists, such as Chopin and Fauré, music was never on the same level as life, but marked out an enclosed garden, a second nature, a magic circle like those consecrated by the augurs, a circle which becomes the imaginary world of art. Music is like a gala, to which one does not go in everyday clothes but dressed in one's best, with a manner of speech chosen to prove that crossing the threshold of the enchanted place takes one into the Other World. Is there anything more unusual than to sing what one has to say, as in opera? This is why the poets visited by the spirit of Apollo express themselves in verse, capital letters and metrical language, bow to the unnecessary restrictions of style and rhyme,[2] in fact put on their dress clothes.

---

[1] Cf. Bizet, *Djamileh*, Danse de l'Almée.

[2] Nietzsche, *The Joyful Wisdom*, aphorism 84; *Beyond Good and Evil*, aphorism 188.

The piano at Montfort.

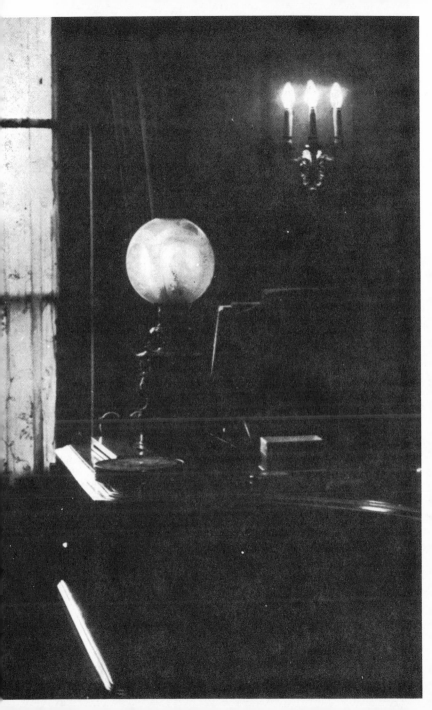

This disinterested need, this urge to affirm, through a special type of conduct, – initiation, *dénouement* and ritual – the retrenchment and jealous secession of aesthetic pleasure, springs from the insularity proper to every work of art. But the spirit of challenge and paradox, together with the taste for formal perfection, take Ravel further still: dismissing romanticism, he cynically professes frivolity and does not want to be profound; while Stravinsky, the avowed enemy of pathetic *espressivo*, paradoxically praises Tchaikovsky, Ravel makes a point of admiring Saint-Saëns. 'The delightful pleasure of a useless occupation', he wrote himself, quoting Henri de Régnier, at the top of the *Valses nobles*. Serious matters can wait until tomorrow. Music is a *divertissement de luxe*, a delightful game, and Ravel, who insists on not spoiling his pleasure, jealously protects this oasis, this 'île joyeuse', against the promiscuities of the century. The happy island, with its high cliffs, enchanted orchards and southern nights, entered the dreams of Chabrier and Debussy as well as those of Baudelaire. 'Là tout n'est qu'ordre et beauté, luxe, calme et volupté'. Unlike the creations of the Romantics this music does not shine throughout the entire breadth of personal existence in order to give it new warmth, but corresponds rather to a series of intermittent escapes beyond reality and life. One can hardly imagine Ravel seated all day at his piano or talking about music in drawing-rooms. When he was not composing the piano remained closed, and his everyday occupations were not those attributed by the popular imagination to geniuses ravaged by inspiration. He used to bury himself in his hermitage when he wanted to compose. Not even illness brought into his music any nervous twists of pain – like those which so cruelly changed Debussy. With Ravel therefore creation represents a disconnected process, a succession of crises which could also be wonderful moments of pause. He has sometimes been reproached for his horror of indiscreet confidences and immodest sincerity, his respect for the 'solemnity' of artistic enjoyment, the kind of Baudelairian dandyism that Roland-Manuel describes with so much subtlety. It would be preferable to trace all this in his taste, his predilections and his way of existence.

Alchimie est art véritable...
Car d'argent fin fin or font naître
Ceux qui d'alchimie sont maîtres.

M. Schuhl, who quotes these lines from *Le Roman de la Rose*,[1] enumerates elsewhere all the pleasant pieces of equipment and automata that we owe to the 'mechanical instinct' of the 18th century, which *non sunt ad necessitatem, sed ad deliciarum voluptatem*: M. de Gennes' peacock, and especially the marvels, the Θαύματα of Vaucanson – the duck which could swim, swallow grain and digest it, the asp, the flute-player, the tambourine player and the timpani player from the Musée des Arts-et-Métiers. And here we are reminded of the 'pavilion of imposture' at Montfort-l'Amaury; Hélène Jourdan-Morhange has described in some charming pages[2] the toys that filled this great toy-box: the Lilliputian nightingale, the bottle-imps, the sulphurs, ornaments, and the little boat that rocked on the waves when the handle was turned. In fact Ravel's ingenuity, unlike that of Leonardo da Vinci, was used not in industrial techniques in the service of humanity but in the manufacture of objects, and especially objects which imitate life. A master of objects – that is how Léon-Paul Fargue spoke of him, and he described his house as a work-box, a case full of precious and precise objects, a surprise toy divided into compartments like the cabin of a boat. Ravel must have enjoyed the Concours Lépine. The thing that attracted him most in the realm of artifice was the creative power of a demiurgic and magicianlike imagination capable of producing offspring that live and move spontaneously. *Homo additus naturae*, man competing with nature and, through a supreme sacrilege, surpassing it, with the result that in the end it is nature, as Wilde said, that imitates art and is in its turn the first artifice . . .[3] a fine cause of pride for the human spirit. 'None of its reputed inventions are so subtle or so grandiose that the human genius cannot create them; there is no forest of Fontainebleau, no moonlight that stage sets flooded with electric light cannot produce; no waterfall that hydraulics cannot imitate well enough to deceive us; no rock that cardboard cannot reproduce; no

---

[1] P. M. Schuhl, *Machinisme et philosophie*, p. 32.
[2] *Ravel et nous* (Geneva 1945), p. 26-28.
[3] 'Artificiel par nature' (Calvocoressi).

On the piano at Montfort.

flower that specious taffeta and delicately painted paper cannot equal'.[1] Ravel would have admired the miracles of the Florentine fountain designers and artificers, the artificial grottoes of the Il Grottesco and the masterpieces of the Rocailleux. It is true that the successors of Chopin had sometimes played with the entertaining stiffness of marionettes.[2] Our contemporaries, setting automata in motion, arranging their *pas d'acier* and *danses cuirassées*, imagine on the contrary that they are being ironical about romantic tender-heartedness: this is no doubt the purpose of Erik Satie's[3] Bottle-Imps, Puppets, Little Wooden Men and Bronze Statues, Maître Pierre's Punch and Judy figures in de Falla, the dolls in *Petrouchka* and even the lead soldiers in Debussy and Séverac. On his side Ravel would consider that no deeper philosophy existed than the wisdom of the ardour that is *'artisan, artificier et artilleur'*, obedient to the skill of our reasons. It is the Baudelairian side of his nature, the cause of the profusion of patent toys, puppets and animated automata that are created and set in motion everywhere in his music by a mind occupied with a mimed version of life. Fabric dolls in *Adélaïde*; a fairytale of steel in *L'Heure espagnole*; and in *L'Enfant et les sortilèges* a fairyland of porcelain, paper and furniture. There are also plenty of hobgoblins and elves in the wood of Ormonde, and the *Ronde* for a cappella choir gives us an entertaining list of them: but these gnomes are mechanical, the elves are wound up with a key; in the magic forest of Chausson, Louis Aubert and Roussel there is a seething population of motorised salamanders and patent birds. For it looks as though Ravel only likes animals when they smell of metal or painted wood; in *Le Noël des jouets* there are painted sheep with enamel eyes and unbreakable rabbit-drums that work; there are Colette's pink lambs and purple goat; the mechanical cricket also in the *Histoires naturelles* which goes tick-tock like a chronometer; and the nocturnal garden in *L'Enfant et les sortilèges* which is no more than a great humming aviary where the squeaking of insects mingles with the music of the toads and the creaking of the branches. The composer-handy-

---

[1] Des Esseintes, quoted by Robert Gavelle, *Aspects du trompe-l'œil* (*L'Amour de l'art*, 1938, p. 238).

[2] Chtcherbatchev op. 15 No. 7 and 41. Liadov op. 29 (*Koukolki*).

[3] *Les Pantins dansent. Ludions. Descriptions automatiques. Croquis et agaceries d'un gros bonhomme en bois. Embryons desséchés* etc.

man amuses himself most of all in *L'Heure espagnole* where there are cuckoos, musical marionettes, and a little cock, and a bird of paradise, not counting the automaton playing the trumpet; above it all the discordant and chiming cacophony of the clocks, which are close relatives to the broken clock in *L'Enfant et les sortilèges*.[1] Ravel liked mechanisms that had gone wrong, and like Satie he must have had a particular liking for pianos out of tune and bleating gramophones. Before Milhaud and Séverac[2] he took a delight in musical boxes and mechanical pianos, as can be seen from the Chinese scherzo in *Asie*, where already we can hear something of the shrill theorbos of the Empress of the Pagodas with their sound of broken walnut shells; in the higher register, like *Laideronnette*, the Fanfare from *L'Eventail de Jeanne* with its rattling bells, me-

---

[1] *L'Heure espagnole* (piano and vocal score), p. 3, 73; *L'Enfant et les sortilèges (item)*, p. 14.
[2] *En vacances*, 1st collection, No. 6; *Sous les lauriers-roses*, p. 25. Cf. Turina, op. 63³. Liadov, op. 32. It is difficult not to remember the *Dreigroschenoper* and *Mahagonny?* In 1917 Stravinsky wrote an *Etude pour pianola!*

chanical scratchings and castanet clicking. From the time of the Feria in the *Rhapsodie espagnole*, the barrel organ from *Petrouchka* could be heard squeaking and grinding. Even where there are no machines, pianolas or musical snuff-boxes Ravel's writing preserves the trace of cog-wheels, as can be seen so well in *L'Enigme éternelle*, which is slightly automatic in its clumsy unhappiness. Automatism already makes its appearance in *Sainte* where the ritual and slightly somnambulistic stiffness of the parallel chords evokes Debussy's dreamy processions of chords and Satie's stiff liturgies. These are some of the signs of this automatism: notes which are reiterated until they lose their breath, imitating the beating of the cembalo as in Manuel de Falla's *Polo* and the last works of Debussy – *Boîte a joujoux*, *Neuvième Etude*, stammering, vibrating, deep-boring notes which penetrate into the soul like drills, and fill the whole of the *Alborada* with their thin staccato; their delicate piercing sounds can also be found in *Scarbo* and the cackle of the Guinea Fowl: this

'Chinoiseries' attached to a door at Montfort.

deafening bird, which is certainly related to Prokofiev's Chatterer, and the gossips, magpies and rogues in Mussorgski, rattles on until she dazes the whole farmyard; above all there is the indefatigable Toccata from *Le Tombeau de Couperin* and the steely *Pantoum* which throbs and spins as dizzily as a motor.[1] After the liking for reiterated notes comes the phobia for *ritardando*, for the *ritardando* is a languor, a tiredness developing into collapse, movement slowing down gradually, then expiring in the prolonged agony and glorious ecstasy of a pause. Organisms pass gradually away as their vital powers give out but automata stop all at once when their spring has run down. Satie, Poulenc and Ravel resist the expiring apotheoses of gradual slowing down because they avoid any affective desire to please. For any *rallentando* shows the overhuman weakness of a being incapable of maintaining its original speed. Thus Fauré avoids the *rallentando* through modesty and Ravel simply because automata are indefatigable. 'Do not slow down'[2]: this is Ravel's unvarying demand in music entirely occupied with composing for itself the imperturbable, indifferent and perfectly inexpressive mask of the engineer: even the *rallentando* passages in the Minuet from the *Sonatine*[3] are in reality a return to the original tempo and not by any means a pathetic collapse, or vigour fading away. The continuity of *rallentando*, like that of crescendo, corresponds well to the eloquent depressions and exaltations of the romantic soul: vigour is gradually subdued, slowed down, and becomes compassionate; as for Ravel, instead of *rallentando* he preferred hesitation, which is spasmodic. The music does not hesitate, but starts off. The dwarf Scarbo makes two or three starts and pirouettes on the spot before leaping into the infernal round; the armchair in *L'Enfant et les sortilèges*, when it is on the point of dancing its grotesque pavane, shakes and shudders like a table that is turning, and its jerky levitation is not unlike the movement of the magic brooms when they begin to move in *L'Apprenti sorcier* or the start of the

---

[1]   Malagueña and Feria from the *Rhapsodie espagnole*, *Tzigane*, Perpetuum mobile from the violin Sonata, *Daphnis*, p. 86, *L'Heure espagnole* ,p. 77, 103 foll.; *Toccata* from *Le Tombeau*, Finale of the Concerto (p. 39, 44) and many Spanish songs by Nin (*El Vito*, *Malagueña*).
[2]   *Le Gibet*, *Alborada* (*Miroirs*, p. 40, 44), *Nicolette*, 2e. *Epigramme de Marot* (*fin*), *Jeux d'eau* (*fin*), *Ondine* (*fin*), *Forlane* (*Tombeau de Couperin*, p. 15), *1st. Valse*, *Scarbo* (*fin*).
[3]   A. Cortot, *Cours d'interprétation*, p. 170–171.

isba with the chicken feet in Mussorgsky's *Baba-Yaga*. After four chords which sound like mistakes divided by silence, Albeniz' *Fête Dieu à Séville* finally begins, like Séverac's carnival *Sous les lauriers roses*, after several drum-beats. This is the cause of the violently disjointed nature of Ravel's music, where the *élan* is suddenly interrupted, especially in *Scarbo* or the *Alborada*; chords do not continue to vibrate in beauty in the apotheosis of the pause but they are suddenly strangled by a sudden silence; or else everything ends with a pirouette or a cheeky gesture as sometimes happens in Milhaud, Satie or Poulenc.[1]

More generally, music which has been bewitched and has the devil in the flesh can only be delivered by a merciful sudden magic spell, the only thing capable of interrupting its perpetual motion; one example is the 'perpetuum mobile' which forms the finale of the violin sonata, or the *Sonate en Duo* in which the first movement is full of insistently reiterated notes. This is how we should interpret the famous modulation into E, the arbitrary 'clinamen' which all of a sudden shatters the spell of the *Boléro*, spurring the music on towards its liberation in the coda, without which the mechanical bolero would constantly be born again from its own self and would dance round in circles until the end of time: such is again the clear-cut resolution by which the action breaks the magic circle of monoideism (which is also a vicious circle) once and for all.

This discontinuity is also found in Ravel's characteristic taste for the marvellous. Ravel's manner is related to spiritualism and also to rhetorical conjuring tricks, which form precisely the sleight of hand, the deceptive trick whereby something that is discontinued seems to continue. One is suddenly forced to admit a certain absurd conclusion and one does not understand how it has been reached, although somewhere there must be a rift or a play on words; for these dialecticians are never wrong in the details, although they are never right in the ensemble. The great phrase in the Andante in the Concerto in G, which sounds as though it was composed all at once, was apparently[2] put together bar by bar like pieces in a puzzle or a marquetry game. To put a rabbit into a hat and pull out cages, wrote Cocteau, is clever.

[1] Poulenc, *Mouvements perpétuels*, II. Milhaud, *Saudades* III and XI. Satie, *Pièces froides* II.

[2] *Maurice Ravel, sa vie, son œuvre* (Grasset, 1938), p. 21.

Ravel au
pupitre
« Boléro »

Only half-measures are unintelligible. This is generally the way genius works, where the before and after can be seen, the creator and the creature, but in fact not the creation; and those who call this action at a distance, this instantaneous magnetism across space, Inspiration, merely gives a name to the mystery. Alchemic transmutation or, as in the pictures of Hieronymus Bosch and Steen, cheating, is the summit of virtuosity for a captious, Panurgic and mischievous virtuosity which is astonished by its own powers. Ravel and Rimsky-Korsakov had a childish curiosity about this working of miracles. It must be added however that Debussy, when he suppressed the discursive mediant in modulation by juxtaposing chords without any transition was the first to create round the tonalities a magic and delightfully suggestive aura, resulting from the immediate attraction of the various presences among themselves. Among Ravel's work special mention must be made of *L'Enfant et les sortilèges* which is a fairytale, a real poem of metamorphoses. In *Ma Mère l'oye*, all through the successive transformations and up to the final apotheosis, the fifths representing destiny evoke, like the philosopher's stone, the fanfares of Tsar Saltan and the incredible marvels of *Sadko*. At the end of the dialogues between Beauty and the Beast the great glissando which ends the enchantment announces the liberation of Prince Charming, who was under a spell. But all the misunderstandings and the comical plot of *L'Heure espagnole* should be mentioned here. Sometimes the magic spells of this conjuror do not achieve metamorphoses but disappearing tricks: 'he looked under the bed, in the fireplace, in the cupboard, ...nobody. He could not understand how he came in or how he got out'. This epigraph for an epigraph, quoted from Hoffmann's Nocturnal Tales, can be read on the title page of *Scarbo*. Scarbo, the wicked dwarf, bursts like a soap bubble; Ondine fades away in showers of waterdrops. We should also remember the long misty trill in which *Le Tombeau de Couperin* spirits away its prelude and its minuet, like the way Debussy ends the *Danse de Puck*, a smooth passage takes up an imperceptible[1] note as at the end of the airy ballet *Les fées sont d'exquises danseuses*, a pirouette, an upward kick, a tremolo... and all is over; no more Scarbo, no more Adélaïde – only a trace of mist on the window panes

---

[1] Cf. *Chanson à boire, Malagueña.*

84

and outside, the mauve moon playing with the clouds. In the same way Chabrier's third *Valse romantique* flies away upwards in smoke. In the same way Snegourka and the Tsarevna from Rimsky-Korsakov's *Sadko* disappear. Disappearances and transmutations – these, therefore, are the two great specialities of Ravel the enchanter: despatch a gnome, hide a poet in a clock, or like Rimsky-Korsakov hide a cossack and a Deacon in a sack and a mayor's sister-in-law in a larder, turn a prince into an ox, make frogs and dragonflies speak... all this is only a game for him; but it can be said of Ravel, the most scrupulous technician on earth, that he carries with him a talisman, a Gygean ring which allows him to compose without anyone knowing where or how. 'Nothing in his hands, nothing in his pockets', states Roland-Manuel;[1] he is like a surgeon who conceals the instruments of his profession in order to look like a bone-setter; he does not dislike being taken for an amateur and although he is exceptionally meticulous, he willingly assumes the disguise of approximation. He wants to look like a charlatan. It is strange that someone who has advocated so strongly, by his technical probity and his scruples, the long patience of labour, should agree to pass for an illusionist, a practitioner in mystery and conjuring.

Instrumental Virtuosity

The fact is that technique, in his magic hands, becomes the instrument of an incantatory action – it might be called a spell. The strange practices of Orpheus, the stratagems for bewitching the listener, are the object of apprenticeship. One is not born a sorcerer, but one becomes one through study. Ravel believed that in all circumstances craftmanship was pre-eminent. 'Naturally you must have the craftmanship';[2] he would willingly deny the 'divine gift', believing with Valéry that inspiration consists in the habit of sitting down at one's desk

[1] *Maurice Ravel ou l'esthétique de l'imposture*, *Revue musicale*, number quoted, p. 18. Cf. Camille Mauclair, *La Religion de la musique*, p. 146.
[2] *Journal* by Jules Renard, p. 1343. Quoted by Léon Guichard, *L'Interprétation graphique, cinématographique et musicale des œuvres de Jules Renard*, p. 179, and C. Photiadès in *Revue de Paris*, quoted article.

every day at the same time; like Edgar Allan Poe, he regarded chance as his greatest enemy. He would certainly have teased Henri Bremond and pretended to side with Alain when à propos Michaelangelo the latter admired the builder's workshop.[1] The conception of genius as ability, and similar intellectual paradoxes fashionable at the moment, would not have displeased him. This was the first cause of his liking for virtuosity, which never changed. This spirit of virtuosity and manual skill, and his taste for solo playing, are surprising in a composer who was not, like Debussy, an especially gifted pianist. It is only fair to recognise that in this he was following a general tendency of our age, which can be found just as clearly in Prokofiev's concertos as in Roussel's opus 36, or the last decorative compositions of Stravinsky after *Capriccio*. Even the latter composer has expressed his intention of taking up again the tradition of Saint-Saëns, that is to say the display piece and concert brio; this intention corresponds clearly with his Scarlatti type of dilettante approach – for music is first of all a 'divertimento', and musical bravura illustrates fairly well this return to 'ostentation' which is the great modern paradox of Baltasar Gracian. Glorious exhibitionism is a relief for the introvert's bad conscience and repressed subjectivity. Technical successes liberate us from the tragedies of our inner life. *Tzigane*, *Sonate en Duo* and the two concertos are dedicated therefore to the glorification of display and show; but the fearsome difficulties of *Scarbo* and the *Pantoum* show also a certain taste for heroism that our joker (what irony of fate!) has inherited from Romanticism, the astonishing performances of Paganini and the prowess of Liszt. Ravel admired the *Transcendental Studies*. The 'solo spirit' leads him to compose an allegro for the harp, a rhapsody for the violin keeps the instrumentalist exposed to view or held like a star-turn impaled on the point of the orchestra, and makes him tread, like a climber on a narrow cornice, over the tessituras most dangerous for his bow; for in the solo and its recitatives there is the ecstasy of the solitude of genius. The bravura cadence finds itself rehabilitated from then on: the cadence in the Concerto for the Left Hand is a magnificent demonstration of power and skill; the cadence in the Concerto in G, a brilliant exhibition for the left hand too, unrolls

---

[1]   *Préliminaires à l'Esthétique*, p. 220. Cf. p. 259.

great arpeggios and emphasises the melody with the thumb below the trills in the right hand; the cadences of *Tzigane* and the Prelude to the Night in the *Rhapsodie espagnole* recall the *vocalises* and the passages for solo instruments, first violin, first flute, solo clarinet, bassoon and harp in the works of Rimsky-Korsakov, *Capriccio espagnole*, *Shéhérazade* and *Great Russian Easter*. The flood of 'little notes', like those that surround Debussy's *Feux d'artifice* and *Poissons d'or*, surround the aquatic and aerial poems of Ravel, *Jeux d'eau*, *Barque sur l'océan* and *Ondine*, *Oiseaux tristes* and the end of the *Noctuelles*, as in the recitative mid-way through the Allegro for harp. Everything is clear, hard and brilliant. The cadences here are no longer vague, as in the abandon and confusion of the Romantic era, but embody something evasive and precise at the same time, something specifically impressionist which is found in Liszt, in the great gusts of *Chasse-Neige*, the twelfth *Transcendental Study*, and in the three poems of *Venezia e Napoli*: *Gondoliera*, *Canzone* and *Tarentella*. The trilled fourths or minor seconds which die away in the upper register in the Hungarian Rhapsodies rustle and melt in *Tzigane* also. We must make a distinction here between vocal technique, pianism and curiosity about the instrument. First, *L'Heure espagnole*, coming after the narrative declamation of the *Histoires naturelles*, so closely modelled on the intonations of spoken language, represent a strange return to the pleasures of *bel canto*. Ravel certainly recommends to the actors all the humility of 'quasi parlando', in other words the tone of recitative and musical conversation; it can be said also that the tone of the final quintet is that of ironic affectation and exaggeration, that this lyricism is not very serious. All the same it cannot be stated that Ravel did not develop a taste for it. The attractive *Vocalise in F*, a romance without words, confirms our suspicions. Thanks to the bachelor Gonzalve, therefore, the finest days of coloratura and flourish[1] have returned; there are *roulades*, trills and runs. Coming after the Mallarmé *Poèmes*, and notably after *Placet futile*, *L'Enfant et les sortilèges* 'sings' a great deal and almost all the time:[2] the voice, instead of staying

[1] *L'Heure espagnole*, p. 19-23 and 102-114.
[2] P. 91 foll. *L'Enfant et les sortilèges* uses a scarcely-sung recitative which must be recited without any intonation. Cf. the shivering, folded, Fauré-like melody mentioned on p. 50 and the spoken recitation of *Chansons madécasses*.

close to the slightest inflections of speech, goes up and down the scale with great strides and indulges in dizzy[1] melodic gaps that had not been risked even in the *Kaddisch*. The declamation is delightful, entirely decked out with pleasant things – falsetto[2], portando, mordents, staccato notes, *vocalises* – and some of these were also to embellish the jubilant *Chanson à boire*. Certainly in the Ronsard *Epitaphe* the voice moves within the interval of an octave, now following the upper notes of the fifths, now slipping into the middle of the fifth in order to fill it with a third... But this humility is, precisely, a further heroic act. Secondly: of all heroes the most virtuoso is certainly the hero of the keyboard because he is sufficient unto himself. From this point of view Franz Liszt, for Ravel, was the incarnation of victory, that is to say resistance tamed, domesticated, made volatile by the technique of man and notably by the technique of the hands; Liszt, like a new Prometheus, stole the fire of art from the dwelling of the gods for the second time and taught men the infinite power of their will; the *Transcendental Studies* assert the manual and digital transcendence of man over matter. It will never be possible to express how much Ravel's pianism owes to the discoveries of this wonderful genius – not only in tonalities and atmosphere, like the E major of the *Jeux d'eau*, or the slightly Swiss romanticism of *La Vallée des cloches*, but first and foremost a barbarous, revolutionary technique which sweeps over the keys like a whirlwind: could *Jeux d'eau* exist without *Jeux d'eau à la Villa d'Este*[3] and *Au bord d'une source*, *Scarbo* without the *Mephisto Waltz*, *Ondine* without *Saint Francis di Paoli*?[4] The end of the *Noctuelles* has echoes of *Saint Francis of Assisi* and *Waldesrauschen*, but also of *Feux Follets* and the *Leggierezza*. It should be pointed out however that with Ravel the search for virtuosity is never merely acrobatic, for it springs always from a purely musical cause: such as the crossing over of hands, which is justified less often by an economy of power than by a certain resonance which must be obtained

---

[1] P. 21. Compare with *L'Heure espagnole*, p. 36, 65, 68-69, 78; for the rôle of Gonzalve, p. 22, 25.

[2] 'Falsetto': *L'Heure espagnole*, p. 48, 53-55, 106-107; *L'Enfant et les sortilèges*, p. 13, 23, 53.

[3] *Années de pèlerinage*, 3rd year (Italy, No. 4). To Liszt, Ravel devotes an article in February 1912 (S.I.M., Concert Lamoureux).

[4] It is not until *L'Enfant et les sortilèges* (p. 26) that a trace of *Wilde Jagd* (Transcendental Studies, No. 8) is found.

Letter dated the 4th August 1923 to H. Jourdan-Morhange.

as in certain passages from Liszt *(Après une lecture de Dante)* which could be played more easily without crossing over the right hand in the upper register, the left in the bass – but would lose the provocative, strange resonance obtained by playing the low notes with the more singing hand, and, by an ironic chiasmus, the high notes with the accompanying hand.[1] Further, whereas each piece from the *Transcendental Studies* represents in general one type of difficulty only (arpeggios, octaves, scales...) each piece of Ravel introduces them all at once: *Scarbo*, for example, is like a diabolical encyclopaedia of all the traps, obstacles and tricks that an inexhaustible imagination can place beneath the fingers of the virtuoso: reiterated notes, trills, alternating chords, rapid runs, the study of staccato notes for the wrist. There is no question of the hand acquiring any habits: *Scarbo*, through the brutal interruptions and continual readaptations that it imposes on the pianist, shatters all the muscular innovations as soon as they are established. Like Balakirev Ravel likes to outline a melody with chords struck alternately by changing over the two hands, as in the *Pantoum*.[2] Like Fauré and Liszt Ravel changes the academic precedence of the right hand; everything, particularly the Concerto in D, shows that he gave

---

[1] Cf. Fauré, 1st. *Nocturne*, and 'trio' from the 2nd *Valse-Caprice*.
[2] *Trio*, p. 18, 19, 20. Cf. *Ondine* and *Scarbo*, *Alborada*, p. 33-34.

ça me sera bien utile : le jour de mon retour à Montfort (le 15), j'ai trouvé lemoyen de m'écraser deux doigts, un à chaque main . Ce n'est qu'aujourd'hui que le médecin a pu me rassurer : l'auriculaire de la main droite, qui jusqu'ici avait tout du bifteck, se recompose ; le médius de la gauche (le plus amoché) toujours insensible, commence enfin à donner de l'espoir : il peut, et doit même jouer du piano, pour exciter les nerfs détruits à se reformer

special attention to the left hand. Like Liszt again, and Mendelssohn, Ravel had a passion for speed, Friskas and 'Gnomenreigen'; but with him a Presto represents lucidity in celerity, limpid speed and not the excitement that astonishes itself and blurs outlines in the drapery of speed and movement. Such is the distance between the romantic *Perpetuum mobile* and the Finale to the violin sonata. Here he comes, this rapid Scarbo, the electric dwarf with his golden bell and his wicked laugh, as nimble as an acrobat and as impassive as a demi-god. He gallops on the wings of the wind among fantastic glissandos and flashes of steel, he whirls round on the spot in reiterated notes, he flies like a firebird from one octave to another. This writing shows rapid thought, nervous control, lightness and the exactness of a clock-maker. The humour is akin to that of Scarlatti, as lively as an elf, leaping from one extreme to another. In this headlong pursuit of ubiquity, fingering disappears. 'Let us find our fingering', wrote Debussy at the head of one of his *Douze Etudes*. Henri Gil-Marchex[1] has clearly shown that Ravel has subordinated articulation as such: in *Jeux d'eau*, *Scarbo*, *Ondine* and the sixth *Valse noble* it is the wrist or even the forearm that strikes the keys as a whole, either by moving up and down or rotating; the thumb is held flat and often strikes two notes at once, thereby causing Scarbo's remarkable predilection for successive seconds; as in the music of Albeniz the pianism is the cause and the harmony is the effect. All this creative writing demands of the pianist a particularly strong attack, fingers of steel, immediate reflexes, extreme delicacy in sensorial terminations, movements as quick as lightning and complete self-control. The keyboard needs both violence and persuasion at the same time, and any clumsiness between these stumbling, incisive figures would be fatal; the pianist sweeps the keys with the back of his hand, striking unexpected resonances from the instrument, through his clearcut attack; the pianist obtains to order the accents of the oboe, the timbre of the cello, the strumming of the guitar and the metallic sound of the harpsichord; at any moment, if it were necessary,[2] he would strike the keys with his fist, exploding with a violent and sacrilegious gesture any prejudice about delicate fingers. For instance, the astonishing glissandos in

---

[1] *Technique de piano* (*Revue musicale*, quoted number, p. 38).
[2] Déodat de Séverac, *Sous les lauriers-roses*, p. 15. Cf. the piano solo version of the Valse, p. 9. H. Villa-Lobos, *Rudepoema*, p. 41.

the *Alborada*[1] – runs of thirds and fourths (allotted to the harps and flutes in the instrumental version), sprays of sound leap up then come down swiftly onto the taut line of the reiterated notes. The arpeggios themselves are played very closely, often descending, and struck as violently as in Séverac's *Sous les lauriers-roses* or in the *Jota Valenciana* harmonised by Joachin Nin. The guitar arpeggio can be recognised in the *Alborada* as in Debussy's *Minstrels*. 'The guitar makes dreams weep' – Poulenc added this line by Lorca above the Intermezzo in his violin sonata; and it could well serve as epigraph to many pieces by Albeniz, de Falla, Debussy, Roussel and Ravel. The resonance of the guitar, which is both arid and convulsive, has introduced into contemporary pianism 'the spirit of a sob',[2] as well as the ascetic and austere spirit of pizzicato. In Roussel's *Sarabande* and *Le Bachelier de Salamanque*, as in Albeniz' *Malagueña* entitled *Rumores de la Caleta*, there is the sound of stifled sobbing. But there is no end to the machinations with which Ravel has enriched the piano, thanks to the industrious agility of his fingers and the fertility of a rhythmic, tactile and instrumental imagination which makes *Islamey* look pale. Ravel's pride in virtuosity, like that of Prokofiev, is due partly to the violence of the post-war period; in any case his music, accompanying the 'step of steel', learned from it something hard, precise and clear-cut, a brilliant resonance giving it a character of its own. Behind the countless details of notation it is possible to imagine inflexible will-power added to the resources of supreme skill which touches off its fireworks knowingly, and assembles or disperses its resonances with exquisite art. Ravel disciplined the tornado of romanticism; the qualities in *Mazeppa* which caused typhoons and the release of natural forces become, in *Scarbo*, artistic violence and concerted cyclone. Thirdly: sometimes pianism can give rise to harmony, and it happens also that contact with the instrument and its raw materials – horse-hair, cord, wood, brass – can fire imagination: this is the reaction of technicalities on the mind, the tool making use of the intelligence in its turn. 'One should not despise one's fingers', wrote Stravinsky,[1] explaining why, from pure pleasure,

---

[1] *Danse du rouet*, *Le Jardin féerique*, *Une barque sur l'océan*, Concerto in G (p. 2), *La Valse* (piano ed. p. 21), *L'Enfant et les sortilèges* (p. 26). Rising and falling arpeggios: Schumann, *Etudes symphoniques posthumes*.
[2] Albeniz, *El Polo*. Cf. Roussel, *Segovia* and op. 20 on the poems of René Chalupt. Falla, *Homenaja* (to Debussy).

he began to work at his own *Piano-Rag-Music*: 'they can bring great inspiration, and when they are in contact with matter that produces sound, they can often awake subconscious ideas which otherwise would perhaps never have been disclosed'. Ravel also wanted to trap the musical phenomenon at its very origin, at the level of vibrating wood or metal. To speak Alain's language, he does not want pure melody taken from grains of resin, fibres of maple or the guts of sheep. And again like Stravinsky, who bought a Hungarian cembalo out of curiosity and used it in *Renard* and *Rag-time*, Ravel was attracted by all sorts of unusual or fantastic instruments: the 'eoliphone' in *Daphnis et Chloé*, worthy counterpart of the 'wind machine' in Strauss' *Don Quixote*, the jazzo-flute, a whistle with slides that sings like a nightingale, the piano-luthéal in *Tzigane*, not forgetting all the ironmongery in *L'Enfant et les sortilèges*, the rattle, the whip, the xylophone; only the cheese-grater is missing, or as in Satie's *Parade*, the lottery wheel and the revolver. Ravel had a very marked taste for percussion: the orchestra for the *Alborada* used kettledrums, the triangle, the tambourine, the military drum, cymbals, the bass drum, two types of castanets, and the xylophone. As for the prelude to *L'Heure espagnole*, it is full of carillons, chiming, mule bells; Glockenspiel linked with the striking of clocks, the sarrusophone, the celesta supported by a drum roll, and everything combined to create a real Argentine cacophony. After *La Vallée des cloches* came the collection of carillons. Ravel always had a weakness for the brass and its metallic fanfares, as in *L'Eventail de Jeanne*. And even *Ma Mère l'oye* seems to include brassy ringing notes. The triumphant fanfares on the piano, in the Finale to the Trio, seem to be written for the brassy voice of the trumpets, and the same may be said of the chimes that celebrate Christmas in the *Noël des jouets*.[2] Ravel also had other instrumental preferences – the flute, the pipes of Pan which, with the horn, was the instrument of Symbolist spleen, the flute that refuses to take any part in emphasis[1], plays more

---

[1]   *Chroniques de ma vie*, V. I, p. 178-179. P. 14, he congratulates himself on composing at the piano, in direct contact with the sound of the music, as Rimsky-Korsakav predicted to him. '*La matière*, that is of prime importance....' wrote Ravel himself in connection with Chopin (quoted by Hélène Jourdan-Morhange, p. 80).

[2]   Cf. the Fanfares by Dukas to precede *La Péri*. Debussy, *Le Martyre de Saint Sébastien*, prelude to the *Concile des faux dieux* (piano and vocal score, p. 47-49).

than once its rustic and smooth melody, first in the andante in *Shéhérazade*, then during the dances of Daphnis, Lyceion and the Nymphs; it is the flute which sounds at daybreak behind the murmuring springs, and it is the origin of the flute that the shepherd Lammon recounts; there is a flute in the small instrumental ensemble of the *Chansons madécasses*, and two in the Mallarmé *Poèmes*, which are reminiscent of certain chamber-music by Albert Roussel, such as *Joueurs de flûte*, Op. 27 or the *Deux poèmes de Ronsard*, for voice and flute, written in 1924.[2] Ravel also liked to use muted trumpets, runs on the clarinet, like Rimsky-Korsakov, and most important of all, after 1919, came the discovery of the jazz band, for Ravel instinctively knew how to exploit its nostalgic resonance and unknown sounds. It is true that Debussy had thought of it first, for the *Golliwog's Cake-walk* was written in 1908 and the finale to the Violin Sonata in 1916.[3] However, the Ramiro theme in *L'Heure espagnole* already had a rag-time rhythm. But most of all it is *L'Enfant et les sortilèges* which makes use for the first time of the blues and the fox-trot, the tricks of the music-hall, typical revue finales and American musical comedy. The scherzo in the Concerto for the Left Hand and the Concerto in G both seem to have been influenced a little by Gershwin. But it must be said that Ravel did not acquire from jazz any state of mind or a specific 'spleen', as happened in the case of the Central European composers, Kurt Weill, Krenek and Schulhof, but he acquired a technique and several tricks of harmonic breakdown, reiteration, duple, throbbing or syncopated rhythms, as in the Blues from the violin sonata, nasal sounds, *portando* trombone passages, neurasthenic saxophone sighs, well-marked or slightly vulgar harmonies; and to end the Andante from the Sonata, the unresolved seventh on A flat, dominant of D flat. Finally, as a supreme sacrilege, the voice itself, the human voice, is used for its own particular timbre, like any other instrument, following the example of Stravinsky's use of the piano in the orchestra. In this way the mixed choir in four parts, singing behind the scenes at the

---

[1] Mallarmé, *Divagations*, p. 159.
[2] A. Roussel, *Divertissement*, op. 6 (1906), *Sérénade*, op. 30 (1925), *2nd Trio*, op. 40 (1929), *Andante et Scherzo*, op. 51 (1934).
[3] *La Rhapsodie pour saxophone* of 1903, an occasional work is more Spanish than Negro. *La Plus que lente* belongs to 1910. With Ravel: *Valse*, p. 21. *Sur l'herbe* (1907).

beginning and end of the first part of *Daphnis*, composes a kind of vocal instrumentation, a human orchestra which adds to the symphony the continuous organ-note of its voices, like the sixteen women's voices in Debussy's *Sirènes*. Like Rimsky-Korsakov Ravel treats each of his instrumentalists as a virtuoso soloist. The families of instruments are emancipated and give up totalitarian unison; the violin is no longer king, and sometimes it is even treated as a mere harp or a banjo, or as a common guitar, while the bow becomes, as in the *Sonate en Duo*, a sort of drum-stick; the strings, played pizzicato, try to evoke the wonderful clear-cut atmosphere of Andalusia, and percussion reigns supreme. The String Quartet is divided as far as possible: in order to play the vast clusters of the recitative, in the *Alborada*, the first and second violins are divided into six, the violas into five, the cellos into four and the double basses into three; and Roland-Manuel in his turn[1] comments on this strange Nocturne from *Daphnis* where a pianissimo drum-roll supports the tremolo of strings, played muted, on the finger-board by an orchestra divided into an infinite number of parts. The result is a fluid kind of writing, and a refinement of timbre which give Ravel's orchestration an indefinable maritime freshness, smelling of salt and the west wind. This lively orchestra, with its adaptable and shattering expansions was once the supple and powerful orchestra of Liszt.

Rhythms

Ravel's discoveries are not limited to instruments; they involve also problems of rhythm, counterpoint and harmony. With him rhythmic strictness is precise and discreet; the spirit of obsession which dwells within him is proof of it, and also his strong liking for dance forms. There is a distinction between polyrhythm, uneven or exceptionally long bars, the cult of 'weak time' and the superimposition of rhythms. Changes in time, which are so usual in Ravel's rhythms, go from simple

---

[1] *Op. Cit.* p. 109. Cf. E. Vuillermoz, *Le Style orchestral de Maurice Ravel,* in *Revue musicale*, quoted number, p. 22.

Letter to H. Jourdan-Morhange
at the time of the violin-piano sonata.

encore pour le concerto.

Pour les gammes chromatiques
en glissé, rien n'est plus facile,
naturellement, sur une seule corde.
L'inconvénient est que, dans l'aigu,
ça commence à être un peu maigre.

Peut-on faire ceci ? (je prends
exprès un exemple où ni le départ
ni l'arrivée ne tombent sur une
corde à vide):

Et, si c'est possible, y aurait-il
plusieurs manières de le faire, c'est-à-
dire de changer de corde ? Pour
l'orchestre, faudrait-il indiquer les

alternation between two different times (for example 6/8 and 3/4 in the *Chanson romantique*, 2/4 and 3/4 in the *Ronde* and the finale to the *Sonate en Duo*,[1] 3/4 and 4/4 in *Trois beaux oiseaux du Paradis*) to a succession of most varied times. Sometimes alternation emphasises the symmetry of a refrain, for example in *Tout gai* where a longer bar in 3/4 time ends each stanza in 2/4. More often polyrhythm is modelled on the irregular accentuation and punctuation of prose on free verse: this is evidently the case in the *Histoires naturelles*, where Léon Guichard amused himself counting the changes of time, which are particularly numerous in *Le Cygne* (14 changes in 39 bars).[2] There is a distinction between this prosodic polyrhythm, which is so noticeably different from the monorhythms of Duparc, and the polyrhythm of expression: in the *Noctuelles* it expresses the frenzied zig-zag flight of the big moths which come blindly up against the walls, flutter round the lights and, drunk with sleep and wandering, come flying limply to alight somewhere on the edge of darkness; in *Petit Poucet* longer and longer bars, 2/4, 3/4, 4/4, 5/4, express the wanderings of the children lost in the forest, trying all pathways one after the other. Whether it is concerned with expression or prosody, polyrhythm in Ravel is nothing more than the scrupulous fidelity to nature, the versatility of an expression which varies with the slightest emotional change; the notes, with their living sensitivity, even anticipate the truth of the words. This detailed and juxtalinear realism, which Ravel shared with Mussorgsky, along with the taste for technical virtuosity, helps to stop any habits from setting in; it forces us continually to readjust ourselves and breaks any rhythmic constellations which might have become encrusted; it prevents the music from drifting into the conventional purring of one rhythm selected once and for all, in fact it keeps us supple by the exercise it imposes on us, it keeps the mind turned towards truth and life.[3] After polyrhythm

[1] At the beginning of the Finale of the *Duo*, exactly 2 bars in 2/4 + 1 in 3/4 = 7 beats).

[2] *Op. cit.* p. 186.

[3] The prelude to *L'Enfant et les sortilèges* is distinguished by the remarkable alternation 8/8, 5/8, 7/8, 4/8, 3/8, 9/8,6/8. Cf. p. 100-101 (4/4, 3/4, 2/4, 5/8). In the violin Sonata (p. 5) the alternation 6/8 (9/8) – 2/4. Cf. once again *Kaddisch* (4/4, 5/3, 3/4), *D'Anne qui me jecta de la neige*, first *Chanson madécasse*, Andante of the *Quatuor*, *Alborada*, *Oiseaux tristes*, *Vallée des cloches*, *L'Heure espagnole*, p. 93.

comes the use of the metronome. Like Verlaine, Ravel always had a special preference for everything uneven, 'plus vague et plus soluble dans l'air'. Perhaps this was partly due to the rediscovery of Greek measures, or to certain Basque dances, like the zortzico in 5/8 time. It is true that to some degree uneven rhythms are the national rhythms of Russian music. Ravel was a great admirer of Borodin and was conscious of the five quavers in the second movement of the symphony he left unfinished. Asymmetric time signatures are typical of the ambiguous arrangement 'ou l'indécis au précis se joint'. The Finale of the String Quartet and the *Noctuelles* are written in 5/4 or 5/8. Between the Quartet and the *Rhapsodie espagnole* and the *Trio* the rhythmic refinement is intensified; Ravel used very long bars more often: 7/8 in the *Martin-pêcheur* and in *L'Heure espagnole*,[1] 7/4 in the delightful dance of the young girls in *Daphnis*, and in *Placet futile*, 9/8, 12/8 and 15/8. The first movement of the *Trio*, notably, shows us an example of a strangely oscillating 8/8 rhythm, already used by Rimsky-Korsakov in *Mlada*[2]; Bartók was to use it in two pieces written in so-called 'Bulgarian' rhythm. Sometimes rhythmic liberty and complexity become so great that all scansion and punctuation seem to disappear; in the second *Chanson madécasse* the rhythms are fleeting and oblique, in the third song they are capricious, in *Barque sur l'océan* they are undulating, then airy in *La Vallée des cloches*, and loose in *Oiseaux tristes*. Like Fauré, Ravel is a master of syncopation. It is normal with him for the end of a bar to cut right through the middle of a phrase,[3] for the melodic accent to be different from the metronomic accent; the composer plays the entrancing game of opposing the rhythm and the natural expression of the melody. In *Noctuelles* and *La Vallée des cloches* the left hand plays in contradiction to the right. The unexpected accents, placed

---

[1] P. 5, 101; 7/4, p. 74; 9/8, p. 79; 9/4, p. 14; 5/4, p. 28, 72-73, 93 and the prelude (p. 1-5). Cf. the *Epigrammes* by Marot (5/4 and 7/4), *Sonatine*, p. 9, *Chanson épique*, *L'Enfant et les sortilèges*, p. 84; Finale of the *Quatuor*, *Sainte* (4/4 + 1/4), *Daphnis*, p. 17 (7/4) and 92-109 (5/4). The final chorus of *The Snow-Maiden* and the one from the 1st tableau of *Sadko*, by Rimsky-Korsakov, are written in 11/4!

[2] *Mlada* II 4 and IV 1 (8/4). Bartók, *Mikrokosmos* VI, Nos. 140, 151 and 153; *Duos* for violins No. 19; *Chants de Noël roumains* I 7, II 6; *Suite dansée* IV.

[3] *Prélude à la nuit* and *Malagueña*, *Pantoum*, p. 15-17, *Daphnis*, p. 30; *L'Enfant et les sortilèges*, p. 1-3.

on weak beats in the Blues from the Violin sonata or the scherzo from the *Sonate en Duo*[1], recall the 'signs of spring' in *Le Sacre du Printemps*; in the *Sonate* deceptive accents give an impression of duple time when it is in fact triple and the contrary impression is created in the *Concerto in G* (where the Andante, with its bass in waltz time, contradicts itself).[2] In the scherzo of the *Concerto in D* erratic syncopated notes float in opposition over basses which remain obstinately in duple time; these rhythmic ambiguities which are found already in the *Alborada*, betray their American Negro origin. Elsewhere, as in the Fugue from *Le Tombeau de Couperin*, delicate or deceptively clumsy accents give the melody an air of suspense, hesitation, a labyrinthine quality that is purely Ravelian; a slight overlapping of tone values is enough here to cast the spell. Metric superimpositions which are true rhythmic counterpoint sometimes give rise to terrible entanglements, for Ravel, just as he liked 'weak time' also liked three beats equalling two. This is simple when the opposed time signatures are related' or have equivalent lengths, one simple, for example, and the other compound; such is the typical case of the scherzo in the Quartet, where 3/4 is superimposed on 6/8; duple and triple times are superimposed in *La Valse*, there are four semiquavers (or two triplets of semiquavers) to one triplet of quavers in *Noctuelles*, three quavers to two triplets of semiquavers in the Prélude to *Le Tombeau de Couperin*, six triplets of semiquavers, two triplets of quavers and four quavers in the final cadence of *Oiseaux tristes*, 6/8 to 2/4 in the Feria from the *Rhapsodie* and the final quintet from *L'Heure espagnole* in which the chorus rhythm is opposed to the habanera rhythm: all these examples still solve equations which are fairly simple; in *Oiseaux tristes* also the opposition of 4/4 and 12/8 is more for the eye and the style than for the ear.[3] The case of the intermezzo to the *Pantoum*[4] is complicated in a different way; here the 4/2 time on the piano (which supposes very long note values) is played beneath the opening bars in 3/4 on the strings; the piano does not have the complete number of bars because

[1] Sonata, p. 13; *Duo*, p. 6-7.

[2] Sonata, p. 25, 30 (and 16-17, 18-19); Concerto, p. 23, 25. Cf. *Daphnis*, p. 41; the 2nd *Epigramme* by Marot and the *équivoques* of the 6th *Valse noble*. On the Andante of the Concerto, F. Goldbeck, art. cit., p. 198.

[3] *La Valse*, p. 2, 3, 4; *Quatuor* (version for 2 hands), p. 16-17, 24; 7th *Valse noble*, p. 18-19.

[4] Trio, p. 15-16. Then the strings adopt 4/2, and the piano 3/4.

they make up exactly eight beats (that is two bars and two thirds of a bar). This causes the apparent independence of the parts and the slackening of all synchronisation; and it is a miracle if at the end the three instrumentalists find themselves together again. But Ravel the chronometrist never loses control of simultaneity, for all this disorder is timed, regulated and adjusted to a split second. There is rarely a cadenza in the proper sense of the term, that is an outpouring of notes without bars where the notes flow and dissolve, liquidating the rules of number and metre and all the geometry of rhythm, reaching the extreme limit of looseness. Metric deliquescence is characteristic of Scriabin, but not of Ravel. There is no 'senza tempo' in the land of harmony, and even the arpeggios of short notes in the first movement of the Trio are 'timed' arpeggios; nothing may enter here if it does not obey the rules of geometry and discipline. For musical time has its laws and even silence, as Alain says, can be counted. According to Stravinsky music is a certain order in continuity, an organisation or construction of sounds based on certain algorhythms. From this point of view the Habanera sums up all

Costumes for 'La Valse' (Derain).

Ravel's preferences, for although it is in 2/4 time the Habanera is the sequence of triple and duple time: a triplet of quavers
followed by two quavers. Precision in uncertainty, evasive
strictness; in this respect Ravel resembles his master Fauré.
But whereas Fauré preferred adaptable compound time, and
especially the fluidity of the barcarolle, Ravel wanted his
rhythms to be commanding, angular and persistent; Fauré
adopted a uniform rhythm for each composition, but Ravel
based his plan with minute care on the slightest natural movements.

Harmony

Ravel's harmony is entirely dominated by an insatiable curiosity which propels him towards the rarest of combinations
and conglomerations. He specialises in chords with appoggiaturas, and especially in the one which falls short of the octave
by a semitone – the delectable, sparkling major seventh. It
is certainly the major seventh, otherwise known as the 'false
note', that permeates the music of Ravel with its acid scintillation,[1] and it is the same interval that vibrates again in the first
Spanish popular song by Manuel de Falla. The relationship
that exists through inversion between the groups of sevenths
and seconds[2] explains Ravel's well-known taste for the interval
of the major second. In the *Alborada* and *L'Enfant et les
sortilèges* the major seventh shrivels up into a minor second.
Possibly the pianistic use of the thumb heightened this preference, which explains the great 'octave seconds' where the
hand is held flat and stretched out full over the keyboard.
Ravel loved the rich flavour of these rugged and incisive
seconds. Sometimes, in *Scarbo*[3] and *L'Heure espagnole*, he

---

[1] *Alborada, Noctuelles, Oiseaux tristes* (*Miroirs*, p. 5, 12, 32); *Concerto in
G*; Concerto for the Left Hand (p. 23-25); *Nicolette*; *Asie*; *1st Valse noble*
(p. 3); *Chanson de la mariée*; *Introduction et allégro* (piano solo, p. 10);
Daphnis (p. 32, 52); *Heure espagnole* (p. 14, 18-19, 30); *L'Enfant et les
sortilèges* (p. 33).

[2] Cf. Bela Bartók, *Mikrokosmos*, No. 144 (Cf. 132, 134-135, 140). *En plein
air*, I and IV (*Musiques nocturnes*).

[3] *Gaspard de la nuit*, p. 37-38. In the same number of the *Revue musicale*
(number quoted, p. 35 and 41) Alfredo Casella and H. Gil-Marchex both
quote this example, the first from the point of view of harmony, the second
from the point of view of piano technique.

102

used them consecutively, in parallel folds and harsh sequences – for he invented passages in seconds just as Liszt invented chromatic octave scales. In *Noctuelles* he prefers to cast them upwards, one by one. More often their ironic staccato can be heard coughing in the bass signifying Belzebuth, the black dog in *Le Noël des jouets*, the wheezing Beast in *Ma Mère l'oye*, Don Iñigo, the fat lover in *L'Heure espagnole*, and the old gallant in *Nicolette*, as well as all the hoarse, lowing, bronchial monsters of Ravel's imagination. To use Satie's phrase the grating seconds are 'as harsh as a nightingale with toothache', and their harsh friction creates a stony, prickly bass for the melody; they are full of thorny, rocky discords. But they can also become smooth and fluid, as in *Jeux d'eau*, *Petit Poucet*, the eighth *Valse noble* and the *Martin-pêcheur*. On other occasions they ruffle the notes with a kind of modest shudder which resembles the goose-flesh of emotion, producing the quivering music of the *Valses sentimentales*. Usually the seconds are found within a chord and flavour it with their hoarse or piquant vibration like a mordent in which the added note continues to sound discordant; this is the cause of the groups of tightly-packed notes in the music of Albeniz which remain hanging from the melody like heavy bunches of grapes.[1] It is possible that Ravel first tasted these slightly bitter seconds in Borodin and more often in Mussorgsky; but most of all they can be found in the sad music of Debussy's last years, in *Gigues* and *Ronde de printemps*, in *Jeux*, the *Boîte à joujoux*, the *Epigraphes antiques* and the *Douze Etudes*, when the writing began to turn into the teeth of a saw, becoming corrosive and cruel, and turning the melody of the violins into scraping sounds.[2] If in Debussy's music the second represents cries of pain, in that of Ravel it is more akin to trembling modesty, for it is the smallest possible interval, making all melody atonal and leaving least room for the development of melody. Beyond the major seventh was the bitonal system, at least for the cynical ear, which is not afraid of deducing all possibilities, even to the extent of absurdity, from the appoggiaturas. Casella has observed that in Ravel's music the appoggiatura is generally resolved over other appoggiaturas; but if we assume that the resolution has been indefinitely delayed nothing

---

[1] *L'Enfant et les sortilèges* (piano and vocal), p. 55. *Chanson romantique. La Valse* (piano solo, p. 9.).

[2] C' K. Szymanowski, *Etudes* for piano, op. 33, no. 2.

prevents us from treating the two extreme ends of the chord as belonging to two heterogeneous tonalities which are developing parallel to each other. This is the case with the piano in the 'perpetuum mobile' from the violin Sonata. It follows that neither bitonality nor even a two-stage polytonality is a particular characteristic of the atonal style, but that it is on the contrary twice as tonal, since it is just as sensuous as polytonality is ascetic; it has kept an affection for the 'reference system', and the fact that its resolution is continually delayed gives it more flavour. Discord is a perfect chord that has been crossed in love; this is the case in those three bars from the *Saudades do Brasil*[1] where a perfect cadence, after several scandalous doings, reveals the voluptuous stratagem of pleasure. But polytonality as such hardly appears in Ravel's music except in the *Poèmes de Mallarmé*.[2] When, for the first time, at the end of the conversations between Beauty and the Beast, Ravel opposes two harmonies which are very far from each other – F major giving gentle protection at the top and bottom, in the centre a dominant seventh which pretends to go towards B, including an A which makes the A natural of F major bristle somewhat – it is with the delicious feeling of playing with a pseudo-danger, and the hope of certain resolution, as certain as the marriage of Beauty and Prince Charming. At the beginning of *Daphnis* the 'theme of the Nymphs' includes over a tonic bass (A) a D sharp which could belong to any other harmony. Ravel carries feigned bitonality to the extreme limit. There is an admirable superbly unconcerned C sharp standing quietly over a dominant seventh on its way towards C major. But there is no need for anxiety, for the two keys come together, as the dance of the Nymphs proves; and there is also this little bitonal intermezzo from the seventh *Valse noble* (above, E, then F sharp, below, F, then G[3]) which ends by an academic F major dominant seventh to which both keys contribute. The most simple case with Ravel, who likes throbbing pedal-notes, is that of an ostinato fixed bass which persists throughout all the modulations of the melody. From this point of view the harmony of popular music, which uses the *musette* and

[1]   Darius Milhaud, *Ipanema* (Saudades No. 5).
[2]   And *Tzigane*, p. 3 (initial cadenza of the violin solo).
[3]   *Vales nobles*, p. 18-19. Thus the friction: C against C sharp, D against D sharp. In *Daphnis*, p. 39, friction of B. flat against B. Cf. p. 89.

the bag-pipes known in Brittany as *biniou* is the origin of bitonality. At the beginning of the Sonata for violin an E flat pedal remains discordantly below a melody in G major, in *L'Enfant et les sortilèges* and *Daphnis* an errant D flat comes up against an obstinate bass in A major.[1] The pedal note is held therefore until the moment when the sparks fly, and it is the ear that over-hears the resolution of the chord while still waiting for it. Bitonality, like polyrhythm, is the extreme limit of independence in the relationship of contrapuntal parts. The prelude to *L'Enfant et les sortilèges* capriciously asserts the mutual tonal and rhythmic liberty of the successive fifths, the melody of the double-bass below and the child's voice. It is not far from here to writing with two key-signatures, in order to create a scandal, and with the Acrobats in *Parade* Satie almost did so...[2] In the Blues the violin plays in G major and the piano in A minor, and the discordant mixture is also an explosive one. This defiance of unity in key signatures can be explained by the need to simplify notation, and as a means of economising in modification and accidentals. But most of all it corresponds to Ravel's keen hunger for inaudible timbres: it could be called the 'bitonality of resonance', a bitonality particularly delectable in those parallel melodic passages in which one seems to be the section or the perspective reflection of the other. They can be heard at the beginning of the *Concerto in G* and in the Cat music in *L'Enfant et les sortilèges*. The flutes in the *Boléro*, doubled by the oboe as though by their shadow, owe to this strange doubling, which is neither unison nor an octave's distance, their unusual profile and a kind of lighting from behind; they resemble the negative rather than the photograph. The cacophony of the clocks at the start of *L'Heure espagnole* is a multitonal cacophony. The two hands play together, one on the black keys of the piano and the

---

[1] *Daphnis*, p. 95-100, 105, 112-113. Compare the cadenzas on the pedal of the *Prélude à la nuit*. *L'Enfant et les sortilèges*, p. 36.
[2] Two key-signatures: *L'Enfant et les sortilèges*, p. 6-8 (where one thinks of *Laideronnette*), 22, 23, 60-61, 70, 82-83, 94; Scherzo from the *Sonate en Duo*; 2nd and 3rd *Chansons madécasses*, *Concerto in G*, p. 51; *Fanfare* from *Eventail de Jeanne*. Cf. Béla Bartók, *1st Bagatelle*, op. 6, which then had the value of an experiment; *Esquisses* op. 9, no. 2; *Duos* for violins nos. 11, 33, 34; *Mikrokosmos* nos. 70, 99, 105, 106. Bitonality is strongly discordant in the 3rd Mazurka op. 50 by K. Szymanowski. Cf. *Masques* III; *Etude* op. 33[3].

other on the white keys, as in the music of Villa-Lobos, simulating the rattle of a bone and an iron bar. Déodat de Séverac knew these resonances well; *Cerdaña* owes them many impressionist effects of mistiness and distance.[1] This proves how cold audacity can lead the most 'tonal' sensitivity to explore the unknown country of ugly, unheard sounds. Something would be lacking in Ravel's language without the cool resonance of the natural eleventh, a wide interval which is like a graceful archway thrown from a tonic to the sub-dominant of the octave above; Ravel owes its use to the harmonic eleventh.[2] It is like an augmented fourth mounted on stilts, and Ravel uses it with an imperceptible smile hovering round his lips. But it would be necessary to quote the whole of *Scarbo* and *Le Gibet*, and *Soupir* from the Mallarmé *Poèmes*, if one wanted to know all the creations born of a harmonic subtlety that has nothing in common with inflation[3]; diabolically complex combinations, chords with compressed and heavily uneven notes, 'chords of chords', Wagnerian curiosities and bland monstrosities all produced by a kind of infinite passion. It is hard to see how the divinely simple musician of the Ronsard *Epitaphe* is able, when he wishes, to simplify his staves or cover them with mysterious logogriphs.

Modes

These refinements explain the marked modal flavour in Ravel's language. André Suarès asserts[4] that Debussy writes more in the major, and Ravel more in the minor. This symmetry seems artificial. In fact Ravel is neither in the major

---

[1] *Cerdaña*, p. 20-21 and 26 (Les Carabineros): Memory of fêtes at Puigcerda.
[2] Quartet, 1st movement. *Entretiens de la Belle et la Bête* (ballet score, p. 22). *Le Grillon, Nahandove*, p. 7., *Heure espagnole*, p. 51, 95-96. *Duphnis*, p. 1, 39, 84. *L'Enfant et les sortilèges*, p. 4, 16, 36, 41, 49, 50, 69, 71. *Sonate*, p. 26-27. *Concerto in D*, p. 9. *Feria* (*Rhapsodie espagnole*, 4 hands, p. 24). Cf. D. de Séverac, *Le cœur du moulin* (piano and voice, p. 139, 152).
[3] *Daphnis*, p. 36, 39. *Soupir, Surgi de la croupe* (*Poèmes de Mallarmé*, p. 4, 11).
[4] *Pour Ravel* (*Revue musicale*, quoted number, p. 7). Roland-Manuel, p. 209: Ravel did not even have the modal training of a Fauré, a Messager, a Saint-Saëns and the Niedermeyer school.

nor the minor; the example of Satie influenced him more than the rediscovery of ancient monody, for he could hardly be regarded as an archaeologist; the rehabilitation of the Gregorian modes depreciated in fact the academic polarity of the major and minor. Nothing is more characteristic in this respect than the uncertainty of the *Sonate en Duo* with the arpeggio of its theme (A) which is minor as it ascends and major when it descends, or else the contrary, and wavers between A major and A minor according to the unstable modulation of its mediant; it is therefore the third which decides as to major or minor. The *Vocalise-Habanera* in F minor, when it passes into F major, keeps its E flat and its D flat; only the third note is raised by a semitone. In the intermediate scherzo in the Concerto for the Left Hand the uncertainty is vertical, that is to say it is bitonal and depends on simultaneity: E minor above, A major in the orchestral bass.[1] The hesitation is usually between the minor and its relative major: this is the procedure in the Trio between A minor in which it opens and C major in which it ends; E minor, in the Prelude to *Le Tombeau de Couperin*, could be G major; and the same thing occurs in the *Toccata*. The two keys G major-E minor in the *Tombeau* and the third *Valse Noble* correspond to the A minor-C major combination in *Ma Mère l'oye*. The right hand in the *Rigaudon* intermezzo plays certainly in E flat major, although the bass asserts the tonic of C minor. In the *Chanson épique* indecision about keys reigns supreme. Sometimes Ravel likes modal uncertainty of a more subtle kind which deceives the ear with evasive precision: in spite of the key signature one could swear that the *Passecaille* in F sharp minor begins in C sharp, and the conclusion on the dominant strengthens this illusion; only a D sharp would convince us, but as though by accident none occurs: up till the seventeenth bar Ravel mischievously avoids this sixth note which would settle the doubt too quickly; from this there comes a very natural inclination to whisk away the melodic accent, which, in the first bar, is on the tonic at the second beat. The illusion is even more complete in *Kaddisch* where it is possible to mistake the dominant for the tonic: a G pedal note maintains doubt about its identity for a long time until the key of C minor openly declares itself. And in

---

[1] B. Bartók, *Mikrokosmos*, Nos. 59 and 103.

L'Heure espagnole[1] there is a delightful modal habanera of which the melody in F sharp minor and the harmonisation in parallel fourths and sixths (then perfect chords) are supported by a B minor bass. There is the same uncertain situation at the start of the melody entitled *Sur l'herbe* between C sharp minor, the nominal, that is to say titular key, and an imaginary G sharp in which the A should be natural. This is more than enough to prove Ravel's infidelity to the sacrosanct dualism of scales. This disaffection itself obviously rendered worthless the artificial modification of the leading note, destined to differentiate the minor mode from its relative key; in fact Ravel only sharpens the leading note through irony, as in the *Chanson romaine* where B natural is obviously an affectation; or through romanticism, as in *Kaddisch*, where C minor demands a particularly pathetic inflection; or finally for the sake of the picturesque, as in *Tzigane*, which employs the same minor scale that gave such pathos to Liszt's rhapsodies. Since the leading note is more or less non-existent in Ravel,[2] as in Fauré, we need only mention the delightful opening of the Third *Valse noble* where D natural appears calmly in E minor with a sort of distant melancholy and faded grace. The indifference of the seventh note to the passionate attachment of the tonic sums up in its way this impassive will which in Ravel is only extreme modesty; it gives to his cadences[3] their inimitable patina, their charm made up of reserve and deceptive stiffness – for even abandon is a measured quality. These statements are never dictated to him by a theory: guided by musical instinct alone he uses modes among which the erudite can identify without difficulty either the Hypophrygian (Ecclesiastical Mixolydian) as in the Third *Mélodie grecque*, where the key of G has an F natural for its seventh note; or the Phrygian, as in the Second mélodie, where it is the second note that is strange (A natural in G sharp); or most of all the Hypolydian, recognisable from the freshness of its fourth note, as in the *Chanson des cueilleuses de lentisques*

---

[1] Piano and voice edition, p. 65. Cf. the *Chanson à boire*.

[2] For example: A with G natural (Pavane from *Ma Mère l'oye*) Pastorale from *L'Enfant et les sortilèges, Trio, Malagueña*: F with E flat (*Trois beaux oiseaux du Paradis, Vocalise, L'Heure espagnole*, p. 94); G with F natural (*Chanson espagnole*): B flat with A flat (*Chanson romantique*); G sharp with F sharp, C sharp with B (Epigrammes de Marot) etc.

[3] Cf. examples of cadences p. 189.

and the *Ronde* where A major permits a D sharp.[1] This causes the indiscreet insistence of the augmented fourth in the *Concerto in D*, the bitonal D sharp in *Daphnis* and the acid D sharp of the *Forlane*.

Counterpoint

Under these circumstances there is a great temptation to define Ravel as the representative par excellence of vertical writing and of harmonic sensuousness. Alfredo Casella himself emphasises most of all his dislike for polymelodic breadth. There is some truth in this. Yet from the time of his youth Ravel showed true contrapuntal virtuosity; it is hardly necessary to recall the skilful, if slightly artificial counterpoint that in *Menuet antique* superimposes the theme of the trio over that of the minuet. Twenty years later, in the minuet from *Le Tombeau de Couperin*, Ravel did the contrary, but with more ease, naturalness and ingenuity, adding the theme of the musette below that of the minuet: here it is the trio that turns into the accompaniment. It is impossible not to admire the counterpoint in Beauty and the Beast, which is very simple, with nothing formal or forced, or the charming octave canons in the *Laideronnette* intermezzo, or the fifths in the *Forlane*.[2] One is reminded of the counterpoint of the rich Jew and the poor Jew in Mussorgsky's *Kartinki*. And even where there is

[1] *Daphnis*, p. 1, 7-8, 16, 92. Cf. *Nahandove* (*Chansons madécasses*, p. 7 and p. 17); Violin Sonata, p. 20-21, 24; *Concerto in G*, p. 49; Concerto for the Left Hand, p. 21-22; Finale of the *Trio*. D with G sharp; Concerto for the Left Hand, p. 24 25; Sonata, p. 11, 16-17, 31; *Daphnis*, p. 74, 77. G with C sharp; *Tombeau de Couperin*, p.23 (Minuet), 24 (Toccata); *Menuet sur le nom d'Haydn*; Sonata, 1st movement, and p. 24, 29, 31; *Concerto in G*, 1st and 3rd movements. E with A sharp; Concerto for the left hand, p. 12-15; *Daphnis*, p. 88, Sonata, p. 20. C with F sharp; *Daphnis*, p. 20. E flat with A natural; *Daphnis*, p. 23. Cf. the admirable subject of the *Fantaisie in G* for piano and orchestra by Fauré. Roland-Manuel considers as the two generating modes of Ravel's melody the mediaeval mode of D (*Menuet antique*, *D'Anne jouant de l'épinette*, *Daphnis*, Duo, Concerto) and the Andalusian mode of E (*Habanera*, *Rhapsodie espagnole*, *L'Heure espagnole*, *Soupir*); secondarily he used defective scales from Java (*Sainte*, *Concerto in D*, *Laideronnette*). The chords would be the projection of this melody onto harmonic order, (p. 213).

[2] *Le Tombeau de Couperin*, p. 12-13. Cf. the *Menuet*, p. 22. *Ma Mère l'oye*, p. 21 and foll.; 35. *La Flûte enchantée*.

only one melodic line, as in *Le Jardin féerique*, no one could mistake the expressive and entirely Fauré-like upstrokes in the bass. Finally in great works like the Quartet and the *Trio* (especially in the Passecaille) it can be seen that the heaviest decorative chords do not exclude horizontal writing in any way. But it is possible to better this, and the choir of animals, at the end of *L'Enfant et les sortilèges*, with its canon-like imitations and its seething superimposed voices reveal a polyphonist worthy of the masters of the Renaissance.[1] Moreover this lover of gratuitous exercises and problems was too fond of anagrams and calligrams not to appreciate some of those contrapuntal amusements which, it must be said, are more for the eye than for the ear; the *Berceuse sur le nom de Fauré* is proof of it, and more especially the *Menuet sur le nom d'Haydn* which attempts various difficult combinations: the right hand plays the theme going up, then the left hand plays it going down, and then backwards: finally the left hand upsets simultaneously the order of the notes which are taken backwards, and the direction of the intervals of the scale, which are taken upside down though they keep their correct distances from the initial B (H) chosen as axis; this mirror-writing symmetry naturally produces an effect which is less auditory than graphic and optic. Mention has already been made of the contrapuntal inversion produced in the Quartet by the mingling of the themes A and C, in the *Allégro* for harp by the collision of C and B, in the Feria from the *Rhapsodie espagnole* by the conflict of C and D, and finally in the *Sonate en Duo* by the continual exchanges between the cello and the violin. Most of all Ravel is a past-master in the art of dialogue between two parts, two fragile and malicious voices, two loquacious monodies which answer each other, talk together and remain both of them suspended between heaven and earth: the Fugue from *Le Tombeau de Couperin*, the *Trois beaux oiseaux du Paradis*, *Rêves*, the *Berceuse*, the first movement of the violin sonata, the duet between the child and the princess in *L'Enfant et les sortilèges* and the entire *Sonate en Duo* vie with each other in proving this unrivalled speciality of Ravel.

Challenge and artificiality: now that these two aspects of Ravel's work have been examined from all angles – instrumental virtuosity, rhythm, harmony and counterpoint, we are seized

---

[1] P. 100. Cf. p. 23 and 35. *Daphnis*, p. 15. *Valse* (piano solo edition, p. 17).

by a doubt – perhaps the technician of so many techniques is no more than a tight-rope walker of genius? Love of technicality, instrumental perfection, manual dexterity and the absolute domination of matter are normally symptoms of decadence. This very adaptability and docility of matter are disturbing, for virtuosity is often only the *virtu* of epigones, just as preciousness is the limit between good and bad taste. The juggler's attitude, which has made the tool completely obedient, toys with difficulties, creates imaginary ones and becomes attached to unusual and worthless trimmings. Behind so much mastery we must discover once more that instinct of the heart without which the whole of music is worth nothing, which, like the inspiration of the Lord, comes not in tempest but in a light breath of air.

Appassionato

'*Where the heart does not enter, there can be no music*'.
(Tchaikovsky)

It is agreed that art is only a delightful falsehood,[1] the most attractive falsehood of all; and that imitation jewels are more beautiful than real ones. It must be said that Ravel did all he could to lend colour to brilliant paradoxes of this kind. He would willingly have said, along with Goethe, that only works of circumstance can be eternal. He often affected to write to order: the *Prélude* composed in 1913 for the sightreading competition at the Conservatoire, *Frontispice*, *Manteau de fleurs*, the *Berceuse sur le nom de Fauré*, the *Menuet sur le nom d'Haydn*, the *Sonate en Duo* of which the first movement was written for the 'Tombeau de Debussy', and finally the *Kaddisch*, without counting the three cantatas, came into existence as the result of circumstances; and even *L'Enfant et les sortilèges*, after all, cannot be said to have arisen from an irresistible and spontaneous creative instinct.[2] His talent and his pride was to compose on a given theme and adapt himself to a convention – this was a new Valéry-like side to his nature. He would have enjoyed working like Haydn and Lully for royal entertainments. 'Harmonic repairs carried out', joked the good Satie[3] one day. 'Remodelling of music a speciality. A symphony? There you are, madam. It is not very entertaining. We can return it to you arranged as a waltz, with words'. The Socrates of Arcueil exaggerated, but Ravel liked to scandalise

---

[1] Alain, *Préliminaires à l'Esthétique*, p. 239.
[2] The *Chansons madécasses*, the *Fanfare* for Mme. Jeanne Dubost, *Boléro* were commissioned.
[3] P.-D. Templier, op. cit., p. 34.

At the hotel of Mamounia, in Marrakech (1935).

people with his humour too, for he was so fond of laughing at romantic fatalism, the fatalism that subjects a given feeling to a given form of expression, indispensable and predestined. With Chopin emotion was born for the piano, and the two were complementary; with Duparc it would be inconceivable to express it otherwise than in song. Ravel laughed at these privileged, indefeasible decisions. Ravel happily transcribed his own works himself, to such a point that it is sometimes difficult to say which is the original version; he did this not only for the pleasure of trying out instrumental colour[1] (a pleasure he shared with Liszt), but also because he did not care whether a piece of music is written for the trumpet, the banjo or the organ. Music is music, and any instrument could serve it as well, bringing out through its own timbre, fingering, and register some unexpected resonance; arrangements 'for various instruments' which a lingering romantic prejudice causes us to regard as sacrilege would not therefore have shocked him *a priori*. *Menuet antique* and *Pavane pour une infante défunte* exist in orchestral and piano versions. The *Alborada* and *Barque sur l'océan* are instrumentalised, and the *Habanera* was written for two pianos before being included symphonically in the *Rhapsodie espagnole*. *Le Tombeau de Couperin* (except the Toccata and Fugue), *Ma Mère l'oye* and *Adélaïde* all became ballets.[2] But sometimes the piano version was the second stage, not the first. Ravel amused himself in arranging the great 1919 *Valse* for piano solo and in this form he created a splendid concert solo as interesting for the hands as the most magnificent transcriptions,[3] such as Busoni's arrangement of Liszt's Fantasy and Fugue for organ, and Liszt's own arrangement of the Andante from the Faust symphony. Ravel the great creator does not despise the instrumentation of other people's music, and his astonishing orchestrations[4], mainly unpublished, should not be neglected.

[1] A. Cortot, *La Musique française de piano*, II, p. 19; p. 45 he makes mention of a piano version of the Allegro for harp which is in fact by M. Lucien Garban.

[2] The *Chansons hébraïques*, *Don Quichotte à Dulcinée* are also orchestrated. Three editions of *Tzigane* exist: for *luthéal*, piano, orchestra.

[3] He himself transcribes for piano solo *Daphnis* and *L'Heure espagnole*, for piano and voice *Shéhérazade*.

[4] Mussorgsky (*Khovanchtchina*, *Pictures from an Exhibition*), Debussy (*Sarabande*, *Danse*, *Epigraphes antiques*), Satie (Prelude to *Le Fils des Etoiles*), Chabrier (*Menuet pompeux*), Chopin (*Nocturne*, *Etude*, *Valse*) and Schumann (*Carnaval*).

Disguises

Challenge plays a great part in these paradoxes concerning conventional music and the interchangeability of different modes of expression. Ravel amused himself, for he had his reasons for exorcising romanticism. He put people off, and distracted our attention like Satie, Stravinsky, and all the great innovators he purposely mislead us. An example is the *Sites auriculaires* (including the *Habanera* of 1898) which through their title alone already evoked the esoteric hermeticism of the symbolists; an element of mystification persists even in the botanic allegory of *Adélaïde*. The Fugue in *Le Tombeau de Couperin*, where the countersubject is the real subject, takes a delight in sending us on the wrong track. There are various instrumental mystifications too; in *L'Enfant et les sortilèges* one could swear that the arpeggios which support the Princess' aria are played on the harp, whereas in fact they are played on the clarinets; in *Le Jardin féerique* from *Ma Mère l'oye* the trumpet fanfares are played on two horns. 'I am made to want a trumpet', says Roland-Manuel: 'not at all, it is a flute imitating the trumpet'.[1] And we can suspect already that Ravel's music, if it expresses something, must express it in reverse, *per contrarium*. Ravel likes *trompe-l'oeil*, false impressions, wooden horses and booby-traps; he wears a disguise; and that is why carnival figures signify for him not the orgies and witches' sabbath of confusion that they signified for Schumann, but pseudonyms, indirect

---

[1] Cf. Cortot, *Cours d'interprétation*, p. 86-87

Caricature by Aline Fruhauf.

incognito, *fêtes galantes*. The anonymity and pseudonymity of fancy dress no longer serve to cover up the unbridled licence of carnival time but to conceal the person with modesty. Puppets and 'suites bergamasques' are not lacking in contemporary French music.[1] Along with Cocteau, Stravinsky, Picasso, Milhaud, Satie and Turina, Ravel found in the frivolity of the circus a means of escape and a change of air; there are signs of this in *Tzigane*, and in the *Alborada* of Gracioso, who is a kind of Andalusian Petrouchka. Extreme intelligence is needed in order to disguise one's own feelings; for it is the intelligence which is the organ of pretence, the indirect approach and the ironic chiasma to which emotion expresses itself no longer simply but διὰ τῶν ἐναντίων. It is possible to study some of these disguises as worn by Ravel.

NATURE

Ravel is first of all a past-master in the art of becoming someone other than himself, and he uses the real world in order to conceal the truth within himself; the knowledge of the exterior, the contemplation of the universe through intelligence, are therefore with him forms of modesty: in fact he speaks of things in order to avoid speaking of himself. With Ravel the world of nature does not reek of cardboard like a theatrical decor, and with him it is the same intelligence that enjoys manufacturing automata or artificial devices and looking at pure facts. Apart from Stendhal, Tolstoy, Rimsky-Korsakov and Mussorgsky, there has never been in the history of mankind an imagination as objective as that of Ravel, as eager for naked truth and life. Sometimes this realism achieves a point of astonishing intensity. This is indeed a fearful modesty

[1] Debussy: *Pantomine*, *Pierrot*, *Fantoches*, *Suite bergamasque*, *Masques*....; Fauré: *Masques et bergamasques*.

Dragon-fly's costume for 'L'Enfant et les sortilèges'. (P. Colin).

Squirrel's costume for 'L'Enfant et les sortilèges (P. Colin).

for which the penalty is such a barefaced
lack of modesty as far as objects are concerned. Harlequinades are not yet necessary:
the naked reality of existences and creatures
can hide this conscience a thousand times
better than the disguises of Cassandra and
Columbine. This is no *fête galante*. It is
the cats themselves which miaow in *L'Enfant
et les sortilèges* through the nasal voices
of two singers 'miaowing' *portando* with
their mouths closed, while round them shudder the strings sliding over the finger-boards;
and later, in the nocturnal garden, the owl
himself hoots through the voice of the slide-
whistle holding discussions with the little
flute that represents the nightingale; in the
depths of the night can be heard the concerted sighing of countless tree-frogs mingled
with the buzzing of insects, the croaking
of toads, the murmuring of branches and
all the mysterious dialogues of the creatures
of midnight. Bela Bartók[1] also creates for
us furtive whispering – mysterious turns,
crackling seconds, high strident octaves,
notes strangely reiterated – which answer
each other and increase in silence from one
end of the night to the other; the fine
rattling of the cricket echoes the rustling
branches, the sighing toads, and the metallic
tick-tock of the beetles. In Ravel's music
little animals and insects compose a kind of entomological
rhapsody. In the whole history of lyricism throughout the
world there is perhaps only *The Frogs* of Aristophanes and
Léos Janacek's *Adventures of Reynard the Fox* which can compare with the pantheistic choir of Ravel's creatures. Behind
the sounds of the animals we can hear the laughter of the breeze
and the creaking of the branches and the deep, sylvan, imme-
morial sound that comes from the throats of the trees and
all the plants in April; there is something heartbreaking about

---

[1]   *Klänge der Nacht (En plein air,* IV) 1926.

this leafy *portando*, and the sobbing wood. So, in Bartók, is the amelodic, atonal, premusical sound of nature, from the depths of which will rise the measured and melodious song of mankind, which is music; so in Liszt is the confused twitter of the swallows with which the expressive voice of St. Francis of Assissi will converse. René Chalupt[1] has reported that Ravel had planned to set The Little Flowers of St. Francis to music. We can hear the cricket from the *Histoires naturelles*, the Peacock which cries 'Léon', the Kingfisher and all Jules Renard's birds whose cackling and squawking was to be imitated in *L'Heure espagnole*. For the artist imitates nature not only by fabricating her sounds but in transporting them in entirety into the orchestra; on one side there is the puerile cheeping of the imaginary birds in *Petit Poucet*,[2] on the other the real songs of birds as in *Oiseaux tristes* and at the beginning of *Daphnis*. At the end of the third act of Rimsky-Korsakov's *Mlada* the chaffinches greet the dawn as in *Daphnis*. These harmonies which are literally imitative[3] with a minute care for detail are clearly at the opposite end of the scale to onomatopoeia which is entirely typical of literary, conventional and oratorical convention; the lowing sheep of the Pastoral Symphony, bookish Georgics and other forest murmurs are no more. Ravel's predecessors were the naturalists of the eighteenth century, Couperin and Daquin, and ·a whole tradition of realism culminating in the birdballets of Liszt, Rimsky-Korsakov and Mussorgsky, and the smooth nightingales of civilised music, the nightingale of Granados' *Goyescas*, and the melodious nightingale of Stravinsky's Emperor of China, the muted *roulades* in Debussy's *Fête galante*, and the atonal *vocalise* of Szymanowski's nightingale. It must be said that Ravel does not record feeling around sensations, like Fauré, nor sensations about things, like Debussy, but the things themselves; it is nature itself, with its colours and its smell of damp grass that figures in this music, live nature in flesh and blood, and not through the intermediary of any person. We can touch her and smell her, we can feel her present and living in matter as in creatures;

---

[1] *Ravel au miroir de ses lettres*, p. 261, 264. On the love of Ravel for birds: H. Jourdan-Morhange, p. 31.

[2] *Ma Mère l'oye*, ballet score, p. 27 (cf. p. 40). *Daphnis*, p. 74. 3rd *Chanson madécasse* (piano and voice edit., p. 16).

[3] The laughs of *Daphnis*, p. 25, 30.

she is present, if not in the botany of the *Valses nobles*, at least in the zoology of the *Histoires naturelles*. This is the cause of the capricious lack of continuity in a diction which spreads through the details of nature with a kind of juxtalinear precision; the cause also of the microscopic and meticulous realism in the description of things. Analysis of Ravel's landscapes shows great variety: misty landscapes still in *Miroirs*, and in *Gaspard de la nuit*, landscapes which are deeply etched and more fantastic. There is every type of night: the voluptuous perfumes of an Andalusian night in the Prelude to the *Rhapsodie espagnole*; at the opening of the second part of *L'Enfant et les sortilèges*, which is a scene of 'jazz in the night', the moonlit garden is full of whispers and sighs – because the darkness, for Ravel the nightbird, far from stifling any presences in its shadowy cloak, strengthens the myriad subdued sounds of creation. The nocturne in *Daphnis*, at the start of the third tableau, is full of more continuous and more fluid murmurs, but it is in reality the end of a night, a dawn glinting with dew. Elsewhere there is the start of a night: in the *Gibet*, set to words by Aloysius Bertrand, the crimson twilight creates round the scaffold of Montfaucon a background that evokes Gustave Doré. At the end of *Le Grillon* and the third *Chanson madécasse* the setting sun casts a light that is not so red; for those two evenings Ravel chose the great nocturnal and Fauré-like key of D flat major. But there is a calmer majesty in the chords that evoke Jules Renard's entirely visual image – 'in the silent countryside the poplars are like fingers pointing upwards to the moon'; and more humility for commenting on Parny's words – 'the wind on evening rises, the moon begins to shine through the trees on the mountain': a Hypolydian G natural brings the coolness of the southern wind through this tropical twilight, motionless and silent. After the nocturnes, dreams of air and the play of water. *Oiseaux tristes* is a static poem and hovers in the motionless air. *Noctuelles*, on the contrary, which is simultaneously a nocturne and an airy picture, comes close to the lightest *leggierezza* of Liszt and Debussy; the latter's *Exquises Danseuses* and the former's *St. Francis preaching to the birds*, the gnomes dancing in circles, the leaves of the forest shaken by the wind, are no lighter than Ravel's nocturnal moths. The water poems proceed in their turn from *Jeux d'eau à la villa d'Este*,

119

where Ravel's laughter soars gaily already in a thousand little crystalline bells.[1] The foaming Ondine laughs out aloud among the undines, while the fountains murmur in the garden at night. In the pointillist music of Ravel the great streams and fountain jets of Liszt break down into showers of drops; everything sparkles, gleams and scintillates, and all the silent amethysts of night can be seen glinting in the depths of the garden; even the musical phrases, touched by the archaism of the harpsichord, are broken down into notes and take on a certain subtle and delicate grace. Ravel is economical with the pedal therefore, for the use of the pedal means vagueness, mistiness and diffluent continuity. But it also happens that in the liquid element Ravel finds again the principles of legato, the Fauré-like rhythm of the barcarolles and the invitation to sleep; the *Barque sur l'océan* sways over the great heaving waves that rise and fall from one end of the keyboard to the other; slight waves gently rock the schooner in *Asie*, which is no *bateau ivre*, to the rhythm of calm triplets; and as for *Le Cygne*, the white creature of the *Histoires naturelles*, he barely stirs any ripples before him, among the boiling rhythms and gentle lapping of the septuplets. Whether he is recording the eternal cradle-song of the waves, or the cool running of the springs in *Daphnis*, or the games of Amphitrite and the naiads in *Jeux d'eau*, Ravel knew how to evoke the fairies of the sea and water. His music is therefore the music of the open air, the sea winds and the open sea itself.[2] Once and for all Ravel escapes from the 'hothouse of boredom', this unhappy subjectivity of which Chausson remains prisoner:

> *Nous n'avons pas fait ce voyage...*
> *Ce voyage n'est que mon rêve –*
> *Nous ne sommes jamais sortis*
> *De la chambre de nos pensées.*[3]

---

[1] *Jeux d'eau, Barque sur l'océan, Ondine, Le Cygne, Asie.* With Debussy *Voiles* (*Préludes*, 1st book) is a suggestion of rhythm, *La Mer* a study of waves. Gabriel Dupont, *La maison dans les dunes*, Nos. 2, 6, 8, 10.

[2] The wind: *Grands Vents venus d'outremer*. The forest: *Ronde*. Pastoral: *Petit Poucet, L'Enfant et les sortilèges*, 1st movement of the violin Sonata, 3rd *Chanson madécasse*, Gabriel Dupont, *La maison dans les dunes*, No. 4; *Heures dolentes*, No. 8.

[3] A. Gide, *Le Voyage d'Urien.*

On the balcony at Montfort.

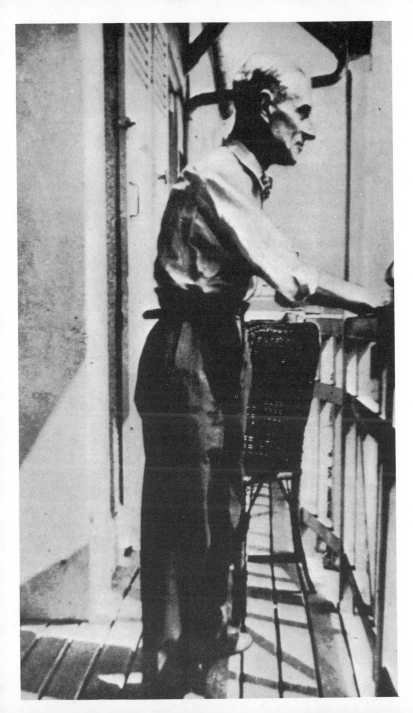

Ravel certainly left this room. But we must realise that happy objectivity with him is only the disguise for his inner secrets; next we must realise that travel and humour will help him to conceal even this objectivity. For just as the stuffed birds in *L'Heure espagnole* and *Petit Poucet* compete with real birds in *Daphnis* and the *Histoires naturelles*, so Ravel enjoys grasping the world after it has passed through fantasmagoria or exoticism. The objective man *a fortiori* can be the illusionist. Like the Swan in the *Histoires naturelles* therefore Ravel pursued vain reflections and fished for clouds; he did so at a time when the impressionists preferred the reflections of things to the things themselves, the filmy and rippling appearance of reality to reality itself, phantasms in the water[1] to solid objects, the shadow of trees in the pool to the real branches. The baroque and symbolist title *Miroirs*, reminiscent of Debussy's *Reflets dans l'eau*, *Images* or *Estampes*, and Fauré's *Mirages*, seems to depreciate the model to the advantage of a secondary reflection. But while the subjectivist, when he comes out of himself, finds only himself, Ravel plays hide and seek of his own free will. For such are the three stages of his ruse, the three alibis of his modesty: naturalism helps him to conceal himself, exoticism to conceal this naturalism and pastiche to conceal this exoticism.

EXOTICISM

This music which for forty years took us from Palestine to Madagascar and from Persia to Spain resembles a fine cruise full of wonderful adventures and delightful encounters. Ravel's 'exoticism' in fact is explained not by a feeling for picturesque colonial scenes or the cult of folklore, and not by a feeling akin to Gauguin's search for lost innocence, but by the extreme mobility of an intelligence capable of assuming any role and of entering into any character. Roland-Manuel describes it as an exoticism without local colour. Ravel can be more Spanish than Manuel de Falla: when he speaks Hebrew he is as Jewish as Darius Milhaud and when he enters the gypsy caravans he can be as Bohemian as Liszt.

---

[1] Τὰ ἐν τοῖς ὑδασι φαντασματα: Plato, Republic VI 510 a.

He certainly shares this polyglot spirit with many of his contemporaries; with all their master-mariners, from Rimsky-Korsakov to Roussel, French and Russian music felt nostalgia for distant horizons and they welcomed invitations to travel.[1] The Asia of Persia and the Caucasus, just as they had attracted Rimsky-Korsakov and Balakirev, inspired *La Péri*, which was written seven years after *Shéhérazade*. Damascus, Persia, India and China were to be the Asiatic ports of call for the new Sindbad. But on the whole Ravel rarely leaves the shores of the Mediterranean. 'I should like to sail away with the schooner', he sings in *Asie* to the words of Tristan Klingsor, but although he was a good sailor the schooner did not let him sail much further away than Fauré, and he did not visit a much more fabulous East. He is one of those travellers of whom one would like to say, as was said of Jules Verne, 'he never went there'. His attention was attracted to Greek music by Hubert Pernot's collection and the harmonisations by Bourgault-Ducoudray. Spain in particular was not merely an entertainment. In the wardrobe of Ravel's disguises this one was not like the others. Ever since the slightly literary Spain of the *Pavane pour une infante défunte*, the Romantic and very Victorian Spain of Hugo, Théophile Gautier, Manet, Lalo, Chabrier and Bizet, he never ceased to

---

[1] Cf. the six passionate *Poèmes arabes* by Louis Aubert.

The fête at the home of the Cad of Telouet, near Marakech, given in honour of Ravel.

be passionately attached to the Spanish disguise. He loved every aspect of Spain – the passionate Andalusia of the *Alborada*, where the shrill arpeggios gleam like daggers; in the *Rhapsodie* there is the exuberant Catalonia of the Feria and the ardent precision of the dances of Malaga; there is the Baudelairian indolence of the *Vocalise* from Havana, the popular nostalgia of the *Chanson espagnole*, the obsession of the *Boléro*, the libertine fantasy of *L'Heure espagnole*, and in *Don Quichotte à Dulcinée*, the courteous, warlike and gallant Spain of the 17th century. Even the most astonishing Spanish effects of Debussy, *Ibéria*, *Soirée dans Grenade* and the *Puerta del Vino*[1] look pale next to these fiery images, in turn arid and intense, scorched by the sun like the landscape of Castille. If Déodat de Séverac, the native of Languedoc, was the poet of Catalonia, Ravel, whose origin was Basque, identified himself with the very essence of Spain. De Falla has admitted that even the Spaniards have imitated him, just as it is said that sunsets imitate the paintings of Claude; and the admirable *Nights in the Gardens of Spain* would certainly not have existed

---

[1] Not counting *Lindaraja*, the *Scherzo* from the *Quatuor*, *La Sérénade interrompue*.

without the *Feria* and the *Prélude à la nuit* from the *Rhapsodie espagnole*. Towards 1924 Ravel disguised himself as a gipsy. Adélaïde, who was in turn a gatherer of lentils, the sleeping beauty, the watchmaker's wife in Toledo, and the Madagascan Nahandove, wanted to camp out one night with the gipsies in order to test her adaptability: for the gipsies belong to Hungary and romanticism, not at first sight to Spain and the Cante jondo. Everything which attracted Ravel towards the music of Spain, the clear-cut outlines, the nervous precision of the rhythms, the classical and entirely Latin purity, and most of all the ardent conciseness which is one of the aspects of asceticism, all this must have separated him from the raggedness and untidiness of the gipsies. In their music, rhythm dominates everything, but it is veiled in a kind of chromatic mist capable of every type of treachery. Unlike other races, the gypsies have no fixed folklore of their own: they possess only one mode and certain types or genres within which the improvisator enjoys the greatest possible liberty, playing developments and variations to suit his fancy, and then forgetting what he has played. These adventurers have no traditions; they are nomads and have no worldly possessions; they have no homeland, and they waste whatever they find; they even abandon their music to the four winds. It is not surprising that this proud careless attitude attracted Liszt, who was a pathetic pilgrim himself and did not detest the music of the open road. But how did Ravel, who represents discipline and hard matter, come to fraternise with tramps?

PASTICHE

The East, Spain, gipsy wanderings, not forgetting the Viennese background to *La Valse* and the Negro period – these were some of the wrong tracks along which the composer decided to direct us. Things were even more complex than this and Ravel even pretended to pretend. Not only did objective truth enable him to hide personal truth, but he used one objective truth in order to deform the other objective truth; he sought historico-psychological truth in apocrypha, reality in anachronism, good taste within bad taste, the charm of outmoded things. It is as though he looked at geography

125

In the boudoir at Montfort.

through history – he is like a historian who takes less interest in Platonism proper than in the figure of Plato as seen by the magicians of the Middle Ages, the pantheists of the Renaissance or the aesthetes of Oxford; instead of a background he preferred to look at the background in the refracted light of the taste* or style of another age. Instead of Vergil in Latin he would certainly have preferred Madame Dacier's translation. This is camouflage multiplied by itself. The period Ravel chose for his prism was usually the 18th century: he had always preferred it to the Renaissance, the Empire, the Louis-Philippe period and the Second Empire, and it had been made fashionable by Verlaine and Henri de Régnier. When Ravel looks in the direction of Madagascar, he sees it through the prose-writing of Evariste Parny, and if he had written an opera on *Shéhérazade* he would have used Galland's translation of the *Thousand and One Nights*. The Chinese element in *Ma Mère l'oye* is reminiscent of Boucher's pictures just as Mozart's Turkish effects are reminiscent of the *Lettres Persanes* and the whole 'alla Turca' exoticism

126

which belongs very much to the time of Louis Quatorze. The 'Bergamask' background in Fauré expresses a nostalgia for the unreal; with Ravel it expresses, just as much in the *Pavane pour une infante défunte* as in *Ma Mère l'oye*, the will for concealment, alibi and uprooting. Even the Minuet which honestly considers itself 'antique', as though antiquity had lasted until the time of Louis XV, is more like the Cythera of Watteau than Greece itself; therefore it is the Minuet that counts, and not its description. But reality is not always refracted through the medium of the 18th century, as the false Javanese colour of the *Pantoum* shows. A close look at the *Tzigane* would certainly show that it was a little tainted with hispanism;[1] instead of a Hungarian rhapsody it is a fine Spanish rhapsody, or almost as Spanish in its way as Debussy's Rhapsody for Saxophone, which should have been somewhat more Negro. But if the *Tzigane* rhapsody is a little Spanish (just as Liszt's Spanish rhapsody is in a sense the nineteenth Hungarian Rhapsody), then *L'Heure espagnole*, in its turn, is rather Italian, with its *vocalises* and ornaments; one can say, it is true, that it is like Domenico Scarlatti, the Neapolitan who became Spanish. But how then can one explain the romantic Spain of the *Pavane*, which is like a picture by Velasquez seen through the eyes of Liszt? What is more, a pavane is neither Spanish nor funereal. And, as though Léon Bakst had realised this desire for an alibi, even the Greekness of *Daphnis et Chloé* is a little tainted with Circassia, Scythia and Sarmatia.[2] The Spanish and oriental impressions of Balakirev in their turn have a very slight Slavonic accent, and their charm consists perhaps in this very lack of authenticity. This search for the refractive medium would certainly explain the backward-looking affectation which is so characteristic of Ravel's taste: and can sometimes be found in the choice of poets – Marot or Ronsard[3] – sometimes in the background to the action, as in *Ma Mère l'oye*, *Le Tombeau de Couperin*, the third waltz from *Adélaïde* and the *musette* from *L'Enfant et les sortilèges*, sometimes in the imitation of the fragile and old-fashioned sonorities of the harpsichord;

[1] For example: piano and violin edit, p. 8.
[2] Roland-Manuel tells us that his master saw antiquity through the eyes of the painters of the Revolution, and Couperin through those of Marie-Antoinette!
[3] With Debussy: Charles d'Orléans, Villon, Tristan Lhermite...

on one side is the homage to Rameau, in the Passacaille from the *Trio*, the ceremonial procession of *Anne qui me jecta de la neige*; on the other side come all the Scarlattiana, the minuets for Haydn, Cimarosa and Couperin: – the graceful sonorities of *Anne jouant de l'épinette*, the outmoded badinage of *Nicolette*, the limpid innocence of the *Sonatine* and the *Quartet*. Couperin was for Ravel what Rameau was for Debussy and Dukas, Daquin and the eighteenth century for Séverac, Scarlatti for Manuel de Falla, Ernesto Jalffter and Joaquin Nin, Cimarosa for Malipiero, Claude Gervaise, and the harpsichord composers for Poulenc. All the same it is not merely a question, as in the case of Debussy, of taking part again in a true national tradition, nor merely, as in the case of de Falla, of entering the school of austerity, nor merely a question of embarking for a *fête galante* and a picnic in Cythera: the old forms,[1] the 'classical symphonies' are in fact only a game, one of the pseudonyms used by the humourist, the musician in disguise, to put off the indiscreet and curious. Ravel's music therefore is always more or less a kind of pastiche; not that Ravel often wrote parodies of anyone, like the occasions on which he wrote in the manner of Borodin or paraphrased an imaginary paraphrase of Gounod by Chabrier;[2] but it is true that pastiche is the limit of ironic objectivity for an intelligence which takes on not only background but characters. In this way the *Valses nobles*, through their title alone, are a pastiche of Schumann's *Carnaval*, and the repeated semiquavers in the Finale of the Quartet, quoting the Finale of the first Sonata for piano in G minor, are also in the manner of Schumann. This spirit of ironic plagiarism is well suited to the good humour of mutual parody among French composers:[3] Debussy imitating Monsieur Czerny, Séverac imitating Daquin, Charles Bordes, Albeniz and Chabrier, Chabrier parodying Wagnerian pomposity, Satie imitating everyone, Saint-Saëns himself, in *Le Carnaval des Animaux*, imitating Offenbach, Berlioz, and himself, Ravel finally who so often speaks the language of Domenico Scarlatti – they all give first place to

---

[1] Cf. the three *Suites anciennes* by Albeniz.
[2] It appears that *Myrrha*, cantata for the competition of 1901, was a pastiche of the sentimental operetta style.
[3] The *Portraits de maitres* by P. de Bréville are rather pious evocations 'in the style' of Fauré, V. d'Indy, Chausson and Franck.

the pretence, and second to the romantic notion of their priority.

An uncommon power of assimilation and a penetrating understanding of others is needed before one can enter into the skin of someone else, occupy his place and become the other person himself, *ipse* – Doña Concepçion, Princess Florine or the sultana in a Baghdad seraglio. But to be oneself and in addition the opposite of oneself – that is the limit of intelligent extroversion for a conscience capable of incarnation in its own negation. Contrariness is perhaps the extreme limit of adaptability. Ravel possessed this gift of ecstatic intuition and unitive sympathy which allows an artist to assimilate

129

Costume for Concepçion in 'L'Heure espagnole' (A. Marc).

what is most foreign to him, to incorporate himself in it, to pour himself out into it and forget himself utterly. Ravel possessed not only the capacity for changing all costumes and décors but that of entering into all types of feeling. He who represents supreme distinction knows how to be popular if he wants to be, and knows how to express flesh and blood vulgarity; the burlesque dance of Dorcon is already worthy of the buffooneries of *Choute*; the truculent and typically Barcelona Feria in the *Rhapsodie* and the *Chanson à boire* could outstrip the Chabrier of the *Joyeuse Marche* and the exuberant cheerfulness of Darius Milhaud. 'Tout gai! gai, Ha, tout gai... Belle jambe tireli, qui danse; Belle jambe, la vaisselle danse!' These words from one of the Greek songs in which Don Quichotte already raises his glass to pleasure can be sensed behind the frank, direct, sane gaiety of the *Rigaudon* as behind the final bacchanale of *Daphnis et Chloé*. Similar roles are played by the popular rounds in the Finale to the *Trio*, all through the *Sonate en Duo* and the first movement of the *Concerto in G*. When Ravel decides to be gay he adds no water to his wine, and a fine festival of pleasure could be created by putting together his most Dionysiac pages, Liszt's *Festklänge*, Chabrier's *Joyeuse Marche* and Albeniz' *Eritaña*. In spite of his reserve, Ravel, to use Monsieur Croche's phrase about Liszt, does not refuse to take music onto his knees, and in spite of his refusal to leave anything to chance, he does not detest improvisation. In answer to distinguished vulgarity and stylised intoxication comes concerted improvisation, for everything is worked out, even the lack of direction. When Gonzalve is inside the clock his monologue is accompanied by runs on the harp and slackened rhythms; the prelude to Lyceion's dance in *Daphnis* is played by a free cadence on the clarinet, while several suggestions of earlier themes are tried out and rejected in turn; the preludes to *Scarbo* and the *Chanson espagnole*, the interludes in *Ma Mère l'oye* show the same tendencies. Improvisation, which is a kind of capricious experiment, appears also in the *Introduction et Allégro pour harpe*, where it is a preface without an end, an introduction that introduces nothing. El Gracioso's impromptu 'copla' in the *Alborada* looks forward, with languid twirlings, to the descending triplets in the Recitatives from the *Rhapsodie espagnole*, and above all to the Malagueña and the *Feria*; chromaticism and the approximate quality of

130

the little notes dominate *Noctuelles* and the *Oiseaux tristes*, like the perpetual changes of atmosphere in *Tzigane*: there is the vagueness of *rubato* and *portando*, the languor of *rallentando*, the excitement of *accelerando* and the improvisation of *esitando*. In the final stretto of *La Valse* and the Friska from the *Tzigane*, rhythm becomes excited, it gives way to panic and casts all reserve to the winds. Everything that shocked an honest and scrupulous artist most, indetermination, rhetoric, vague and untidy forms – Ravel adopts all this as a joke and a pretence. To like simultaneously both Castilian reticence and passion that fades into the mists is surely as far as a challenge can be taken. Lack of precision here is only one more type of precision, a refinement of finesse, just as studied negligence is only a form of supreme elegance. This aristocratic finesse is reminiscent of Fauré. Someone who seems to go on looking when he has already found what he wants, who appears to despise details when they have been arranged with precision and who, without seeming to touch them, makes up his chords note by note – these are traits revealing a clever man, a teasing, mischievous man who is as cunning as Ulysses. Finally there is the false grandiloquence, the flourish that clashes so paradoxically with Ravel's nature and its laconic understatement. Ravel never becomes informal without a smile, for he has not only genius but good taste. Also, when he lets himself go

it is always with a grain of salt. Every degree of pomposity is represented, from obvious parody in the Peacock in the *Histoires naturelles*, or in Don Iñigo Gomez, the official personage[1] in *L'Heure espagnole* who also spreads out his tail, to the entirely natural majesty of the Concerto for the left hand. Between these two extremes there is the

On the piano at Montfort.

[1] P. 35 and p. 13 the perfect comic chords on these words: *'l'heure officielle n'attend pas'*. And Debussy, *Boîte à joujoux*, p. 45. Cf. Gabriel Dupont, *La Farce du Cuvier*, act I, p. 54-62 (Arioso de Dame Jaquette).

Chanson romaine, which is the quintessence of pomposity, in a sense concentrated canzone, and many 'menuets pompeux'[1]; sometimes it is impossible to say whether they should be played with humour like the homage to S. Pickwick Esq. and like Satie's caricatures – 'c'est le colonel, ce bel homme tout seul', or whether they should be taken seriously like gipsy fanaticism.

DANCE

It is not true therefore that Ravel's music is divertissement without expression; but its expression is indirect and oblique – we must know how to interpret its moments of reticence, its paraphrases and euphemisms. This is so true that even its impassiveness has become an allegory, a significant figure, the exoteric appearance of hidden intention. The affectation of indifference is just as much a disguise as allegorical simulation or contradictory simulation: nothing is the contrary of something else, it is always something. And this is the reason, as has often been said, why the dance is the natural form of this music – dance which is stagnation, movement on the same spot, violent action which instead of coming out into the world goes back into itself, finds its finality within itself, marks time and goes round in circles; it is action become stationary agitation or, as Alain has said, movement in immobility. Everything turns into jerky movements, meaningless leaps and figures, steps forward followed by pointless retreats. There are ancient dances[2] like the Passacaglia, the noble Pavane, the graceful Forlane, the cheerful Rigaudon of Provence, the Ronde and above all the Minuet. There are romantic dances like the Waltz;[3] American dances like the fox-trots, two-steps and Bostons in *L'Enfant et les sortilèges*. Spanish

---

[1] H. Jourdan-Morhange heard in 1936 an orchestration of Chabrier's *Menuet pompeux* by Ravel (*Ravel et nous*, p. 88).

[2] Pavanes: *Pour une infante défunte*, in *La Belle et la Bête* (to be compared to the one by Fauré, op. 50). Minuets: *Sonatine, Tombeau de Couperin, Sur le nom d'Haydn, Menuet antique* (to be compared with the one in Fauré's *Masques et bergamasques*. Musettes: *Chanson française, Tombeau de Couperin*.

[3] · The *Valse, Adélaïde; A la manière de Borodine*; the Entretiens from *La Belle et la Bête; L'Heure espagnole*, p. 45, 51, 53-54, 86, 88-91, 96-99; the theme of Chloé in *Daphnis; L'Enfant et les sortilèges*, p. 74-81.

dances like the Malagueña, the Boléro and most of all the *Havanaise*, the Cuban Habanera,[1] that is to say the Andalusian tango, which Bizet, Saint-Saëns, Chabrier, Laparra and Louis Aubert have made famous and which was the rhythm for the most passionate accents in *Soirée dans Grenade* and *Puerta del Vino*. Even where this music does not adopt the uniform rhythm of a dance it has a natural tendency to flow into choreographic form: the *Sonatine* is a kind of miniature ballet, so is the Allegro for harp, and the scherzo from the Concerto for the Left Hand; and the *Alborada* in its turn is a real ballet, like *La Valse*, the *Boléro* or *Adélaïde*, like *Daphnis*, *Ma Mère l'oye* or *Le Tombeau de Couperin*, a ballet still waiting for its producer. M. René Dumesnil has observed that the three songs of *Don Quichotte à Dulcinée* form a suite of dances – guajira, zortzico and jota aragonese. Even Ravel's lyricism therefore assumes choreographic form, whereas with Chausson the reverse is the case – his forlanes, pavanes and sarabands are like elegies.[2] It is true that Ravel's dances are always expressive and differ profoundly from the states of mind that they suggest to us: warm and sad sensuousness does not demand a chàconne but a waltz; the habanera is passionate, ardent and precise, and not at all effeminate like a drawing-room tango; each rhythm therefore has its own specific emotional quality. Further, Ravel's dances are expressive not directly through the conventional association of a certain form of music with a certain attitude of the composer, but indirectly through the emotion which is engendered in us. It is not necessary for a composer in a sad mood to write a funeral march if a minuet or a seguidilla, depending on the circumstances, can break our hearts. There is no other way of explaining that *Le Tombeau de Couperin*, perpetuating the memory of friends killed in the war, is a set of six dances which are imperturbably cheerful and serene; or that the *Sonate en Duo* inscribes on the 'Tombeau de Debussy' gay refrains and rounds. It seems strange too to have chosen the name of Gabriel Fauré as a theme for a *Berceuse*. It is true that Fauré in fact showed Ravel how to write 'humoresques' and that Debussy

[1] *Rhapsodie espagnole, Vocalise, Grillon, L'Heure espagnole*, p. 22-24, 25-27, 31-32, 40, 60, 65-67, 82-84, 88, 100, 102-114. Cf. Debussy, *Rhapsodie for saxophone, Lindaraja, Soirée dans Grenade.*

[2] *Quelques danses pour piano*, op. 26. With Hugo Wolf the elegaic, the habaneras become laments: *Spanisches Liederbuch*, no. 21.

himself gave the title of *Gigues tristes* to his first orchestral *Image*. The indifferent speech of Nahandove seems surprising, but the Fauré who wrote the *Clair de lune* in his turn had a habit of putting us off with ironic alibis, by pretending that nothing was happening. In Satie's *Morceaux en forme de poire* and his *Pièces froides*, delightfully tender music, in Stravinsky's *Mavra* as well as in Kurt Weill's *Lindbergh Raid*, 'oratorio-reportage' in fifteen communiqués, with its shimmies and one-steps, the music has no direct connection with the text. Ravel's disguise makes his features immobile and gives the lie to his words, causing him to resemble those ballet figures, for which Derain designed the costumes, in Sauguet's *Fastes*. From the beginning to the end he kept himself rigid in this disguise, from the fine inexpressive chords of *Sainte* (1896) to the dreamy procession of fifths in *Ronsard à son âme* (1924). Dance forms therefore endow Ravel's sensibility with a false apathy, a false anaesthesia, a false ataraxy; it gives him an appearance of frivolous detachment which serves the baffling stratagems of modesty. Dance is the shrouding isolation of his dream.

Sensuousness and Vehemence

'No bites tonight', says the fisherman in the *Histoires naturelles*, 'but I bring back a rare emotion'. What is the inner truth and the message indirectly revealed to us in the dances and humoresques, and in that very objectivism which was intended to hide the message, but betrays it all the same by the suspect attention Ravel gave to certain roles? He is like a lover who wants to show no preference to any one of the women he knows but is unable to conceal the fact that one of them disturbs him. Hélène Jourdan-Morhange has spoken of 'la Fauvette indifférente', 'the indifferent warbler', the title of a melody that Ravel had planned during the first world war. This is Ravel the ironist caught in a trap – he is not Watteau's *Indifférent*, but he is half-indifferent. Don Juan for every woman, except for one. 'But no, you pass by,' sighs the woman in *Shéhérazade* when she sees L'Indifférent, 'and from my threshold I see you go away'; and much later it is the passionate Madagascan who says to Nahandove 'You are going away and I shall languish...' Or as Satie makes the elderly lover in *Colin Maillard* say to an attractive hussy – 'He who loves you stands two yards away. He is holding his heart in his hands. But you pass by without realising it'. They all seem to recall the *Song of Songs*: 'My beloved has gone away'.[1] Ravel has weaknesses therefore, human preferences, and it is when we come across them in a sudden flash that we are able to decipher best his predilections. By a strange dialectical effect, intelligent extremism, at the moment of its greatest coldness, suddenly doubles back on itself. One must not play with fire. If one pronounces the words of love carelessly one risks falling in love properly; if one imitates the *Tzigane* carelessly one risks waking up one morning and finding oneself a gipsy, talkative and undisciplined. In this way the magician has become the victim of his own magic. To become, through study and discipline, the contrary of one's self is a dangerous game for those with passionate natures, and Ravel is certainly not the first engineer who has let himself be taken in in this way. He certainly knew the temptation of forbidden fruit; he was not made of steel like the clocks in *L'Heure espagnole*, but on the contrary he possessed from birth the terrible two-fold sensuousness, both in harmony and melody, that passionate musicians receive in their cradles along with the fairy's kiss. Ravel participates in the comedy that he only wanted to watch; he, the witness, the conscience, the Spanish cricket, the Emperor of the Pagodines and the squirrels, he is moved like any other man. The fine sang-froid and sovereign irony disappear; nothing remains of the sang-froid or the conscious thought: only the confession of a tender heart which is like all other hearts. One should beware of the tarantellas that hover in the evening air round the hills of Anacapri; one should not play with serenades. And if we had any further doubts about this Ravel himself would tell us so. Jules Renard's *Journal*[2] tells us that 'he opposed his own sentimental and instinctive conception of music to d'Indy intellectualism. In fact the great strategist, the rogue, the lover of trinkets, admits that he is sentimental.

[1] Cant. V 6 *Shéhérazade* III. *Chansons madécasses* I (p. 7) Satie, *Sports et divertissements*.
[2] P. 1343, apud. L. Guichard, op. cit., p. 179. Cf. what he says against Brahms in S.I.M., 15th March 1912, Concerts Lamoureux (reproduced in the *Revue musicale*, quoted number, p. 84). Roland-Manuel doubts the likelihood of this conversation with Renard (*A la gloire de Ravel*, p. 73).

135

Elsewhere he makes claims on behalf of the sacred rights of inspiration against the supremacy of craftsmanship and technique. It is not clear whether the impassiveness is a disguise or whether the sentimentality is a mystification.

Alfred Cortot recollects seeing the direction *appassionato* only once,[1] in the first movement of the *Sonatine*. Either he exaggerates or else he has read too quickly: the direction 'passionate', 'with passion' can be found in a hundred other places[2] in Ravel's music, ironic certainly in *L'Heure espagnole*, but very sincere in the Adagio and the Finale from the Quartet, the *Allégro pour harpe*, the Feria from the *Rhapsodie espagnole*, the suppliant dance of Chloé. And it is this word that can be deciphered on the unpublished manuscript of *Myrrha*. Even in places where he dare not pronounce the forbidden word, this word 'passion' that he is longing to write, which is on the tip of his tongue, he hovers round it and replaces it with circumlocutions like 'very expressive', 'with an intense expression'; this can be found in *Tzigane*, the *Alborada* and the Second *Valse noble*. But an intense expression can only be the expression of a passionate heart. This is the reason why, in spite of his wish to remain unaffected, Ravel sometimes gives way, like a simple romantic, to the languor of *ritardando*. Anyone who has never heard the precious *Placet futile* or the voluptuous *Prélude à la nuit* from the *Rhapsodie* cannot know what these weakening rhythms mean in Ravel's music; in Chloé's suppliant dance the tempo slows down every two bars while in certain habanera rhythms in *L'Heure espagnole* it is the last quaver of each bar which is played a little more slowly; and neither is the graceful Sixth *Valse noble*, with its languishing cadences, afraid of approaching the attractive realms of bad taste, this good bad taste which in fact is only our human weakness.[3] It is worth remembering also the delightful emotion which takes hold of the notes in the Second of the Marot

---

[1] *La Musique française de piano*, v. II, p. 32; *Cours d'interprétation*, p. 171.
[2] *L'Heure espagnole*, p. 21; *Daphnis*, p. 64; *Rhapsodie espagnole*, edition for 4 hands, p. 29; *Quatuor* III and IV, edition for 2 hands, p. 23, 32; *Sonatine*, p. 4, *Allégro pour harpe*, *Tzigane*, etc.
[3] *Daphnis*, p. 62-65; 3rd, 5th, 6th, 7th *Valses nobles*; *Heure espagnole*, p. 82-83 (cf. 98), 106, 108-110, 113; *Prélude à la nuit*; *Placet futile*; *Tzigane*; *Sonatine*, Minuet; *Tombeau de Couperin*, Minuet.

136

Epigrammes, when the voice sings 'Dès que je pense être un peu aymé d'elle...'

This thought, ever since the beginning of time, has made hearts beat faster, this thought projects a kind of imperceptible disturbance onto the keys and into the voice, like a slight trembling. No more harpsichord, sang-froid and musical marionettes. Only a player with a heart of stone could play or sing this passage without slowing down. 'Et c'est toi que j'aime', whispers the gay Third *Mélodie grecque*, becoming suddenly tender. In the same way the languid *rubato* from which Ravel only abstains with the greatest difficulty dominates in the *Vocalise*, the Second *Valse* and the ornaments in *L'Heure espagnole*;[1] here, where the true nature of the man is revealed one realised what it cost him to appear impassive. The vague *portando* also plays a great part in the vocal divergences in *Placet futile* and *L'Enfant et les sortilèges*.[2] It must be added finally that Ravel, like Chabrier in the *Habanera*, does not object to doubling his melody at the distance of a few octaves, in order to render it more penetrating; the same thing in Ravel's *Pavane* of 1899 or in his *Habanera* could be explained perhaps by the influence of realism, but in the most sublime pages of the *Trio*, where the wonderful phrase is doubled, the composer does not despise the superimposition of the violin and the cello at a distance of two octaves and the same tendency persists even in *Placet futile*.[3]

Within Ravel therefore there is a Gonzalve who is ashamed of himself, a sentimental bachelor who does not want to be

[1] *Heure espagnole*, p. 79, 111, 113; *Allégro pour harpe* (piano solo, p. 10); *Daphnis*, p. 62-65; 2nd *Valse noble*, *Placet futile*, p. 6; *Tzigane*, p. 2; *Vocalise*; *L'Enfant et les sortilèges*, p. 70.

[2] *Vocalise*; *L'Enfant et les sortilèges*, p. 20 (and 38), 62, 67-68; *Placet futile*, p. 6; *Le Cygne*; *Sur l'herbe*; *Chanson italienne*; *Noël des jouets*; *Heure espagnole*, p. 19.

[3] *Petit Poucet*; *Habanera*; *Pavane pour une infante*; *Quatuor*, 1; *Trio*, p. 5-7, 8-9, and the Finale; *Noctuelles*, p. 5, 10; *Heure espagnole*, p. 43; *Le Cygne*, p. 36; *Trois beaux oiseaux du Paradis*; *Placet futile*, p. 7, 9.

139

moved yet often succumbs. The violent and almost melo-dramatic pathetic element in *l'Indifférent* from *Shéhérazade* admittedly dates back to 1903; two years later in *La Vallée des cloches* this broad flowing insistent lyricism lingers over the keyboard from top to bottom and could not have come from Massenet.[1] But the Dionysiac frenzy of the *Feria*, the sensual fury of *Daphnis* with its leaping exciting bacchanal and the passionate crescendos of the Concerto in G express the very genius of Ravel: in this concerto a kind of lyrical exal-tation sustains the cadence of the first movement, directs the left hand in which the thumb picks out the second theme below the trills of the right hand, then sweeps away in an admirable tutti the soloists' two hands and the orchestra itself. When Satie attacked the romantics in his *Fantaisie musculaire* his ironic direction was 'Fire!' Ravel used any pretext to intoxicate himself with the philtre of inspiration, and irony can certainly take a lot of responsibility: waltzes can be sen-timental, Gonzalve in *L'Heure espagnole* can be a figure of fun, *L'Enfant et les sortilèges* can contain a parody of music-hall. But there is no parody in the Passecaille, and Chloé's suppliant dance, with its realistic touches, its ebb and flow of vigour, is not ironic but very serious. The 'copla' in the *Alborada*, with its ornaments and *rubatos* is also serious; the voluptuous intermezzo that interrupts the *Feria* is more serious still, and its melody, after various modulations and grace notes droops languidly over its lower tonic F sharp; this music, like the *Prélude à l'après-midi d'un faune*, is truly the poem of perfumes and the aphrodisiac summer. The tonadilla and the cadences thus represent an oasis of idleness in the midst of sarcasm. The paganism of *Daphnis*, the oriental eroticism of *Shéhérazade* and the mystic exaltation of *Kaddisch* are more than enough to rout the frivolous gallantry of *Adélaïde*. Along with the disguises, the commonplaces of contemporary critics can now fall from the composer; he was thought to be subtle, but nobody thought him great; he was described as a goldsmith, a jeweller, a confectioner and expert in 'little things'. And there were many remarks about the cerebral and small-scale quality of this art. Yet for a goldsmith there are many moments of *appassionata*. For Ravel was not only the

---

[1] *Miroirs*, p. 46-47: compare it, for the curve, with the melodic line of the *Trois beaux oiseaux du Paradis*.

drum-major of the *Noël des jouets* and *Laideronnette*, the orchestrator of toy-trumpets and almond shells: he was also the composer of the grandiose Concerto for the Left Hand, and of *Tzigane*;[1] the conductor of the crickets' orchestra is the composer who intones in the Finale to the *Trio* this colossal hymn where there is so much to admire at once, the richness of the harmonies, the natural sense of greatness and the irresistible breath of inspiration. The Trio is indeed sublime, the masterpiece of this generous heart. The emperor of ladybirds, it must be said, was not narrow-chested after all. Beyond the atoms and the toys, beyond even the distant horizon, the vast pianissimo that ends *Le Grillon* gives us a glimpse of the night spread out infinitely far over the countryside. The man who was nearsighted enough to tell us of the grasshoppers and the vixens possessed also the most regal and pantheistic sense of distance.

This power can become passionate and excited enough to reveal strange depths of violence in this humourist. The rebellious side of his nature reveals a ferocity that is worth examining closely. He had attacks of sudden violence, wolfish anger, normally revealed in two savage discords slapped against each other, an aggressive shout, a roar. 'Aoua!'[2] Beware of the white men who live along the shore', cry the free Madagascans, rising against their tyrants. And the child in *L'Enfant et les sortilèges*, like Madame de Ségur's[3] Sophie, echoes them: 'Hurrah! I'm free, naughty and free'. At the other end of the score the cries of animals united against the children of men correspond to the revolt of the Child against family discipline. Even in *Daphnis* there is the barking of the two hoarse syllables during Dorcon's dance, the Pirates' dance and the final bacchanal; and finally it is the call of Scarbo, the wicked imp of midnight.[4] This call expresses a revolutionary protest against order, tradition and law, a revolt of nature against the very limits that the artist imposes on himself, a libertarian claim for solitude. *Aoua*! down with the bourgeoisie and their official honours. Even in the Guinea-fowl and the *Sonate en Duo* there

---

[1]   *Tzigane*, p. 12 (piano and violin). 'Grandioso'.
[2]   Cf. Examples p. 189.
[3]   A. Cœuroy.
[4]   *Daphnis*, p. 23, 25, 58-61, 95, 105-106, 108-109, 112. *L'Enfant et les sortilèges*, p. 9, 87, *Scarbo*, 2nd. *Chanson madécasse*. Cf. the cry of the Peacock and the Cricket.

are moments of rage which cannot deceive us. But they are only quarrels. It happens too that the Madagascan, instead of rejecting civilisation, becomes confused; in addition there is the stormy romanticism of the *Grands vents venus d'outremer*, the fanaticism of the *Tzigane*, the intoxication of the *Alborada*, the violence of *La Valse*, the breathless conclusion to the *Boléro*, so characteristic of the anguish, distress and yearning of the post-war period. But nothing is more astonishing than this divine anger when it is in the service of pleasure, when it emphasises life instead of seeking obscurity: there is the marvellous spitefulness of the *Rhapsodie espagnole* with its orchestra full of thundering broadness of sound and infinite caresses; for its vehemence contains the electric suppleness of a cat and the savagery of a force of nature; the orchestra is in a tearing, leaping rage, it is supple and cruelly vicious, but it has moments of ineffable sweetness – the union of fury and sleep, said Jacques Rivière. Grace and power, the emblem of French music, the qualities that were also the secret of Liszt, in his sublime Mephistopheles and the *Faust Symphony*. The nymph Ondine weeps and then laughs. The entire paradoxical nature of Ravel is contained in this alternation of confession and humour, in this will to control a heart that nature had designed to be impetuous and vehement. This dispute seems to be summed up in the conflict between the two themes of *Scarbo*; A, wearing seven-league boots, climbing up and down with big strides; B, pirouetting on the spot, representing vigour that is stilled.

The *Alborada* is the same, an ambivalent aubade with a strange association of geometry and passion, humour and tenderness. The clock-maker knows very well what snares lie in wait for him, and he takes many precautions against the demons of complaisance. First, the 'interrupted serenade', where development is stifled. 'Take hold of eloquence and wring its neck'. *L'Heure espagnole*, with its delightful habaneras that whet the appetite and then stop short, consists

142

entirely of a series of interrupted serenades, it is a collection of sketches. The aubade of El Gracioso also begins a sentimental refrain at every step and abandons it the next moment, leaving us puzzled, while the bassoons laugh up their sleeves; just as we were going to take the piece seriously it has flitted away, like Saint-Saëns' graceful *Trio* in F major which fizzles out with a negligent stretto, or like the end of Satie's second *Air à faire fuir*, or Poulenc's second *Mouvement perpétuel* which ends with a glissando and a cheeky laugh. Perhaps this is what the narrator of *Shéhérazade*, at the end of *Asie*, calls 'interrupting the tale with art'. Ravel preferred rhapsodic variations with their popular songs and dances to symphonies. Sometimes Ravel ends a piece, but instead of introducing suspense he cuts it short; in this way a laconic asceticism, miserly conciseness and a kind of melodic Malthusianism represent a second kind of interrupted serenade; this can be felt very clearly in brief masterpieces like *Là-bas vers l'église*, the Third *Valse noble* and the serenade of *La Flûte enchantée*, where Ravel listens with beating heart to the melodious voice of the sirens, the forbidden song, and wonders if he dare go on. With him this extraordinary reserve is not so much a stratagem to incite our appetite as an antidote to literary amplification, phraseology and automatic droning on; the result is that the apparent lack of continuity in diction with Debussy and Ravel consists in fact of a terror of declamation and in a reduction to essentials, the deflation of redundancy. The same thing is true of the Mephistophelian simplification in the third part of Liszt's *Faust Symphony*. A great deal of heroic abstinence is needed in order to stifle pathos in this way. It is purely this modesty that differentiates Ravel from Liszt, for Liszt's serenades are rarely interrupted, and once he has started he cannot easily be stopped. The curtailed crescendo represents a third form of interrupted serenade. In Ravel's music there are certainly crescendos which become progressively excited, as for example the musette in the minuet from *Le Tombeau de Couperin*. The *Boléro* is nothing more than the study of a gradual crescendo in which the successive degrees are viciously measured out, with a kind of inexorable phlegm; the *Valse chorégraphique* contains both kinds of crescendo, the continuous crescendo which becomes gradually intoxicated until it is quite dizzy, and, fifty-four bars before the end, the Forte which is brutally interrupted by a pianissimo. In the *Alborada* the nerves are rudely shaken by these explosive crescendos, which are very short, taken up roughly and as eruptive as the clown himself. The interrupted serenade becomes also the school of sobriety, for it expresses in fact the collapse of ideals in life; while the Cricket represents irony finally transfigured into poetry the Swan indicates rather disappointment, that is to say poetry stifled by the prose of everyday life: Lohengrin's pure Swan becomes merely a fattened goose; the white winged creature is no longer as white as all that, the white bird is only a fowl; the chaser of clouds is only an eater of slugs; the swan is no more distinguished than a guinea-fowl. Just as Satie's 'carrier of big stones' lifts with a great effort a ton of rock ('It is pumice stone'), so the fisherman of reflections 'has caught nothing', and the pomposity of the Peacock signifies the fiasco of grandiloquence. Alas, the bride will not come today. In the piece entitled *Golf*, from Satie's *Sports et divertissements*, the colonel, who is a clumsy sportsman, misses his shot and breaks his club: the ox becomes a frog. One must not therefore accept the words if one wants to be immunised against disenchantment. This is the purpose of the arid staccatos in *Scarbo* and the *Pantoum* which pierce the cloud of romantic pedalling; like Debussy, Liszt or Prokofiev Ravel knows the incisive and caustic value of the low notes used in pizzicato;[1] he has learnt that they prevent us from being taken in and that they prepare the way for bitter disillusionment; staccato notes, bursting open empty swelling, hasten the deflation of inflation.

These two sides explain the easily-recognised double aspect of Ravelian melism – lyrical effusion and amusement. First of all come three types of melodic outline which are truly related to each other – the generous curve of *Soupir*, the penetrating poetry of the sirens' song in *Ondine* and above all (may the clocks forgive him, although they have no heart) this powerful unheard song which rises from the earth at the opening of the third scene in *Daphnis* when the sky grows pale in the east and the whole of nature wakes and stretches round the sleeping shepherd.

---

[1] Cf. *Malagueña*, Dance of Dorcon in *Daphnis*, *Chanson espagnole*, *Alborada* (*Miroirs*, p. 33, 42, 43). The chord of the second achieves the same end. Cf. Debussy, *Boîte à joujoux*, *En blanc et noir*, *Jeux*, *Douze Etudes*.

Ondine

Daphnis

Soupir

'Singing pleases my soul', says the third *Chanson madécasse*. The long phrase in the adagio from the Concerto in G, with its pathetic leading notes, the Princess's aria in *L'Enfant et les sortilèges*, *Kaddisch* even, are evidence of the inexhaustible gifts of nature and a melodic inspiration which is perpetually renewed. But there is a second type of melodic line, more graceful and more futile, not at all the generous flow of *Daphnis*, but an exquisite badinage with a frivolity playfully emphasised by caprice and repetition. What antinomies could exhaust the charm of this old-fashioned freshness, the subtle and learned naïveté? The divine, indefinable qualities of Fauré can be recognised in it, but there is some other element. The tender melodic line is simultaneously popular and refined, evasive and precise, distant and close, naïve and precious, with an elusive distinction even in childishness itself; it recurs in countless forms in the French rounds in the *Sonate en Duo*, the themes of the Quartet and the *Sonatine*, in the Third *Valse noble*, the pastorale of *L'Enfant et les sortilèges*, the intermezzo of the *Rigaudon*, the *Beaux oiseaux du Paradis*, the *Berceuse sur le nom de Fauré*, without counting *Laideronnette* and the *Pavane* from *Ma Mère l'oye*; even the Andante from the noble Concerto in D and the Adagio from the Concerto in G sing a childlike kind of song. This is the profile that is at the same time ingenuous and voluptuous, sentimental and violently poetic, and it is such that a musical ear would recognise it among a thousand. It sometimes happens that an imperceptible melancholy, like a mist of tears, clouds these divertissements; playing the *Sonatine* or the Fugue from *Le Tombeau de Couperin* one's heart sinks and one does not know why; in the same way the counterpart to Chabrier's *Joyeuse marche* is *Mélancolie*, the second 'Pièce pittoresque' where Manet's Olympia comes to life again; for as Baudelaire was fascinated by Lola de Valence, Chabrier met the fixed stare of falsehood, the large black, sad eyes of Olympia. This is a noble sadness of life which emanates from humour in

146

general and from the discretion that an impetuous heart must impose on itself. It is this that we can feel through the repressed ardour of the *Sonatine*, in these dissimulations, shudders and cabrioles, and in this whimsical and distant air that it assumes in order to speak to us. In the end modesty is stronger. Ravel then designs for himself a disguise that is most carefully imperturbable, in the hope that nothing can be seen through it; he makes himself more unkind than he really is. What can be done in *Nahandove* to prevent tenderness from revealing itself below the exoteric concealment of affected indifference? 'Without any variation', can be read above *Sainte*: and in the trio of the *Menuet antique*: 'Without any accentuation'. Above the melody that fills the middle part of *Le Gibet*,[1] intensely lyrical but without any *ritardando*,

---

[1] *Menuet antique*, p. 4; *Gaspard de la nuit*, p. 19; *Sainte*. Cf. *Barque sur l'océan* (*Miroirs*, p. 24). Satie, *Mercure* (*Le Bain des Grâces*). Poulenc, *Mouvements perpétuels* I ('incolore') II ('indifférent'). *Napoli II* (Nocturne). *Suite in C major* (Andante). Milhaud, *Saudades* IV and V.

he writes, paradoxically, 'without expression'. This phrase is so poignant and pathetic that it is deeply moving. Either Ravel is laughing at us or else, like Satie, he is merely pretending to be indifferent. The more deeply he feels, the more he affects a colourless and politely uniform tone.

Anti-romanticism with Ravel therefore was a reaction against the romantic that he might have become if his will had weakened. There are other romantic things besides the first song in *Don Quichotte*. The slightly Gothic aspects of *Gaspard* are certainly only pastiche and background: neither is *Le Gibet* a scene from Hoffmann, nor *Ondine* a Lorelei, nor the fantastic night of *Scarbo* a Walpurgis night. In fact Ravel is much closer to the Mendelssohnian type of presto than to Schumann[1] moonlight, and the incredible imaginative mobility of *Gaspard* is completely different from the clumsy and over-serious *Kreisleriana*. Ravel practises a different type of skill from the Teutonic bourgeois. But his dexterity masks a pathetic inner life. Ravel represents repressed desire, reticent friendship, strength that does not show all its power at once. Ravel is no Jekyll and Hyde, but like the Harlequin figure in the *Alborada* he is a motley, fantastic and contradictory characater. He is frivolity and ardour all at once. 'In art', said Debussy, 'one usually has to fight only against oneself, and those victories are perhaps the finest of all'. What is known as Ravel's taste, this delightful taste consisting of proportion, denial and exquisite discernment, this good taste is perhaps only bad taste that has been stifled, the knowledge of bad taste, and of good taste, and of himself – indulgence nipped in the bud by scruple. Even vicious preciosity is a game played with bad taste. All the heroism of bad taste can be found in the conscience of the implication known as renunciation. If Ulysses knew how to avoid the Sirens, Ravel, like Déodat de Séverac,[2] sometimes listened to the 'Naiad of Banyuls'. These are the games of love and humour. Reason and passion – or rather half-way between the two, with an utterance that is perpetually interrupted – these are the qualities of the *Alborada*, and of the whole of French music.

---

[1]   Roland-Manuel attributes to him Variations on a chorale by Schumann, a youthful experiment, and the orchestration (unpublished) of *Carnaval*.
[2]   *Sous les lauriers-roses*.

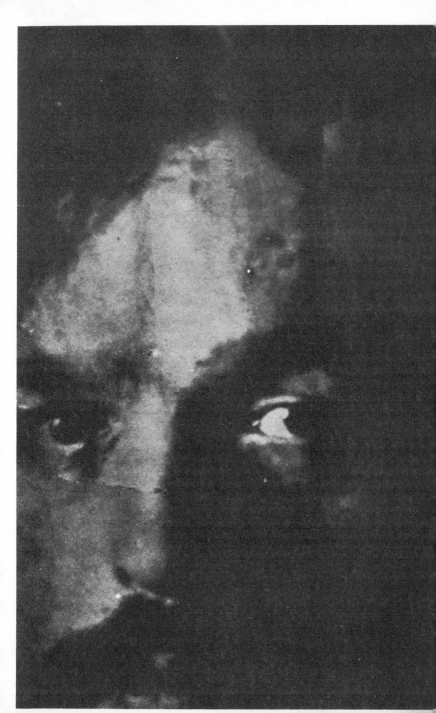

At this point we should be able to separate the world of Ravel and the world of Debussy; the comparison has been made many times,[1] and with the very legitimate desire to differentiate where their contemporaries had sometimes failed to do. It is very possible, since the desire for improvement can spoil a good thing, that the tendency today is to invent points of opposition and split hairs; for if a little lucidity helps to differentiate between these two great creators, more lucidity brings them closer together. On the level of technique the differences are incontestably great. Throughout his life Debussy remained faithful to the pantonal scale and the various modified chords and augmented fifths which arise out of it. With Ravel there is practically no trace of the six-tone scale, and one hesitates to describe in this way the very vague tendency of *Jeux d'eau* or *Barque sur l'océan* to progress by whole tones. The major sevenths belong to Debussy; but the major second is also common to them both, like the habit of introducing discords without either preparing them or resolving them. The essential point lies not in this, but rather, as M. Mantelli has shown with such acute precision, in the quality of the discords themselves, which are more liquid in Debussy and more static, hard, and closed in on themselves in Ravel. This is the cause in the *Valses nobles* and *L'Enfant et les sortilèges* of immobile appoggiaturas and the chords without issue which mark out the realm of discord; it is also the cause of bitonality, which arises from the petrifaction of the 'wrong' note; with Debussy, in the *Boîte à joujoux*, *Rondes de printemps*, *Ibéria*, *En blanc et noir*, *Pour les sonorités opposées*, bitonality expresses poetically the co-existence and copresence of all creatures, and creates a harmonic atmosphere in which the chords, grasped in their evanescent state, vibrate, shudder and penetrate into each other with a divine type of ambiguity. It is helpful to compare the versions of Ravel and Debussy of the Mallarmé *Poèmes*. The first surprising thing is that they differ only in the choice of a text for the third melody, for which Debussy preferred the indolent *Eventail* and Ravel, who always enjoyed difficulties, chose a sonnet that is completely hermetic. Ravel's setting of

[1] Roland-Manuel, *Maurice Ravel et son œuvre dramatique*, p. 17-20; Alfred Cortot, *Musique française de piano*, v. II, p. 15-22; Alberto Mantelli in the *Rassegna musicale*, 1938, II, p. 63. In the number *Ravel* of the *Revue musicale*, the articles of André Suarès (Pour Ravel, p. 7), Emile Vuillermoz (Orchestral Style, p. 23), Alfredo Casella (Harmony).

Debussy (photo taken by P. Louÿs).

Soupir uses many more notes than Debussy's, the vocal melody is very firm and rests on clear arpeggios that seem to gleam with metallic light. To the same words Debussy wrote a kind of Verlainian madrigal; the vocal melody is more thoughtful, and often unaccompanied, floating over gentle vague soft chords which brush against us like a caress. In the same way *Placet futile*, in Debussy's setting, is a delicate minuet in muted colours, a sort of rondeau through which pass shimmering light gruppetti of demisemiquavers, barely touching the keyboard. The address 'Princesse', goes down with Debussy, up with Ravel. The latter, after a fairly long prelude for the piano alone, unfolds a precious, baroque and rather Gongoresque melody which twists the vocal line, imposing wide intervals on it but preventing it from trembling. The pianistic background, from which the major seventh stands out, is as rich as it is clear-cut. There is only one passage which the two composers have treated in the same way – they both harmonised the words 'Chez tous broutant les voeux et bêlant aux délires' with parallel sevenths made up of thirds piled on top of each other. The same impressions would strike anyone who listened one after the other to Debussy's anxious, voluptuous Sonata in G minor for piano and violin and Ravel's limpid Sonata in G Major. It is fascinating to compare the dazzling *Ondine* of *Gaspard de la nuit* and the Debussyist Ondine of the second book of *Préludes* with her gentle scintillation, irridescence and air of relaxed abandon, or to compare the two Toccatas, the one from *Le Tombeau de Couperin* which spins and hums like an engine and hammers the keyboard mercilessly, with that from the Suite *Pour le piano* which is more capricious and feminine, with indefinable swooning vibrations round the notes. One can also see the differences between Debussy and Ravel through comparing the vague and misty Spain of the *Sérénade interrompue* and the brilliant Andalusia of the *Alborada*, or by comparing the homage which both composers paid to Haydn: Debussy wrote an undulating whimsical waltz which is all improvisation, Ravel a graceful and deceptively old-fashioned minuet, which is the pastiche of a pastiche.

Between the orchestration of Debussy and Ravel the differences are also imperceptibly slight, but very revealing: the former writes with more nonchalance, grey shadows and softer tones, the latter with more metallic sonorities, more clearcut rhythms, a more incisive and arid melodic line. The result is that Debussy's orchestral work demands a kind of re-creation from the interpreter, while Ravel's orchestra limits the initiative of the instrumentalist and permits only the faithful execution of what is written. The popular airs, in *Ibéria* – fragments of habaneras, distant music – are like frayed rags floating dreamily at the edge of night; but in the *Rhapsodie espagnole* the popular songs march along in an angular way, and they appear in entirety. *Fêtes*, the second *Nocturne* for orchestra, like *Feux d'artifice* in the second book of *Préludes*, evokes a vague Quatorze Juillet, softened by misty distance, broken down by our dreams; but the petulant Catalan *Feria* from the *Rhapsodie* is blazing with sunshine. It is not Ravel but Debussy who sought gardens in the rain, Scotch mists and autumn by the sea. There is no poetry more all-embracing than this Debussyist poetry of vague and fragmentary suggestion; it takes hold of the listener and breaks his heart. But where instrumental colour is concerned nobody can rival Maurice Ravel.

Even the use of forms reveals the differences between them. Somewhere André Suarès compares Ravel's dances and Debussy's *Préludes*; the prelude is a picture of atmosphere, vague and fugitive, and the title even is added afterwards, to prevent the pianist's imagination from becoming too hidebound. Ravel, unlike Debussy, accepted without difficulty the discipline of the classical forms, sonata writing and the handling of themes: the Trio, the Quartet, two Concertos, two instrumental Sonatas and a Sonatina for piano indicate sufficiently his taste for the logical strictness of thought. *Daphnis*, with its architectonic pretensions, refutes Monsieur Croche, who laughs at the studious game of symphonies. This game pleases Ravel, like all games, and notably exercises in counterpoint. Even the poem of *Jeux d'eau*, which is a kind of fresco, has two subjects and a re-exposition like a sonata. It is not that Ravel cultivated a development, and occasionally he would conceal the traditional plan; just as there is an Aria and a Burla in Schumann's Sonata in F sharp, a Mazurka and an Intermezzo in Balakirev's Sonata in B flat minor, so the Scherzo in Ravel's Trio is a Pantoum and the largo a Passacaglia; in the same way the andante in the violin Sonata is called a Blues and the finale is a Perpetuum mobile. But Ravel appreciates construction and we know that he would seek out unnecessary

153

restrictive gymnastics in order to make himself supple. The very different evolution of these two creators sums up clearly their opposed natures. Ravel goes straight to his goal and with him the inevitable period of searching is reduced to the minimum. The nonchalant Debussy dawdles much longer, with his fearsomely sensitive skin, his exceptional sensitivity and the 'kind of vegetable spontaneity which according to Mantelli characterises his discoveries. Ravel left no stones unturned, he took advantage of everything, everywhere: in Schoenberg, Wiener, Doucet, and the Musée Grévin. Ravel exploited and took advice, but Debussy made only chance encounters and his reaction was passive.

And yet Ravel's art has few particularities which could not fit in just as well with Debussy's art. In fact Debussy is Ravelian just as Ravel is Debussyist. Ravel can be more Debussyist than Debussy, as can be seen easily from the *Martin-pêcheur* in the *Histoires naturelles*, where the vague outlines already suggest *Brouillards* and *Feuilles mortes*. And when talking of mist we should remember the conclusion to the Eighth *Valse noble*,[1] and also the end of the Minuet from *Le Tombeau*, where the design loses its relief and its contours. *La Vallée des cloches* and *Oiseaux tristes* are to *Miroirs* what *Le Cygne* and *Le Martin-pêcheur* are to the *Histoires naturelles* – an impressionist aesthetic approach and a certain technique of blurring and haze. And there are many Debussyist elements in the springtime music of *Daphnis*.[2] If *Estampes* had an influence on *Laideronnette*, the *Jeux d'eau* in their turn perhaps influenced *Estampes*, just as the *Rhapsodie espagnole* influenced *Parfums de la nuit*.[3] Most noticeably of all the famous pedal-note from the 1895 *Habañera* vibrates throughout *Lindaraja* and right on into *Soirée dans Grenade*.[4] It is

---

[1]   For this end, cf. Debussy, *Placet futile* and *Pour la danseuse aux crotales* (from the Epigraphes Antiques).

[2]   *Laideronnette* is played on the black keys like *Pagodes* (Cortot, p. 43). On the other hand one can scarcely see what the beginning of *Le Gibet* owes to the *Hommage à Rameau* (Roland-Manuel). It appears that the cantata *Alcyone* was inspired by Debussy's Quartet. *L'Heure espagnole*, p. 34, 40: an innocent parody of Pelléas? Ravel ardently defended *Rondes de printemps* and *Parfums de la nuit* from *Ibéria* (*Cahiers d'aujourd'hui*, 1913, II). *Daphnis*, p. 3 and 31.

[3]   *Jardins sous la pluie* (Cortot, p. 31; Gil-Marchex, quoted article. H. Jourdan-Morhange, p. 61). Cf. *Jeux d'eau*, p. 3, for a sign prophetic of *Sirènes*. *Ibéria* II, 44-49.

[4]   Léon Vallas, *Debussy*, p. 232. Louis Laloy, *La Musique retrouvée*, p. 167.

possible that the hardening of the notes in Debussy's later works, from the *Images* for orchestra to *Jeux*,[1] was largely accomplished under the influence of Ravel. Debussy, with the younger composer close on his heels, seems to have hurried to become anti-Debussyist; the wonderfully hard steely construction of the *Epigraphes antiques* and the *Douze Etudes* reacts against 'Impressionism' before the advent of *Les Six*.

All that Ravel needed, in order to equal Debussy, was to have come before him. They were both torn by the same passions: on both sides there are exceptionally delicate sensory terminations, an absolute realism and a taste for immediate fact; and like the Madagascan they both possessed extreme sensuousness and violence. Viñes represented Debussy as a mediaeval adventurer who could also have been a condottiere, a poisoner or an architect. Debussy fought against his desires and instincts but in fact the tidal wave often swept him away: and that is why he got so much more out of life, why he was more productive than Ravel and why his creative inspiration was more vehement, more uninhibited and more generous. But as far as craftsmanship, taste, and technical mastery are concerned, then Debussy was so unequal that he was only an apprentice in relation to Ravel. Sobriety with Ravel went so far that it might almost have become sterility. Through modesty and restraint who knows whether this extreme conscientiousness and sovereign irony would not have dried up the river of melodious song? His wrath against 'detestable sincerity, mother of prolix and imperfect works' is well known; no doubt it is to sincerity that he imputes the demonstrative chatter and all the shocking waste of emotion that ruins sensitivity, debases language and finally depreciates the true instincts of the heart. Nietzsche admired in Sophocles the half-visible quality of feeling, and this quality belongs also to Ravel. Something of the modesty possessed by Racine, Malebranche and Pascal – the phobia about introspection, the horror of autobiography and intimate revelations – lives again in this classical figure. 'Words are detestable'. 'The ridiculous idea of painting his own portrait'. He shared this objectivity

---

[1] P. 17-18 of the piano score, of which the subtle *accumulations* are reminiscent of the *Histoires naturelles*. Cf. *Le Martyre de Saint Sébastien*, p. 57 (p. and ch.).

155

with Rimsky-Korsakov. But in him modesty is combined with affective lucidity. 'I can see clearly into my heart'. One thinks again of the love-strategy of Adélaïde, and especially the delightful *marivaudage* of Beauty and the Beast, with its unemphasised confessions, its moments of coquetry and its repressed burst of vigour, and at the end, everything is sorted out; there is a resemblance with Musset's comedy *Il faut qu'une porte soit ouverte ou fermée*, where there is the same two-fold action conducted between two very lucid hearts which see through each other very clearly, pretend to be indifferent, advance and retreat, and keep a firm control over their ardours. 'Love and reason are only one thing', states the *Discours sur les passions de l'amour*. 'Poets therefore are wrong in telling us that love is blind; the bandage must come off from his eyes and he must enjoy his sight once more'. So much finesse, combined with so much intelligence, supposes centuries of amorous civilisation, and a well-developed sense of the things of the heart. But Ravel has a lover's quarrel with sincerity. Fortunately the imposter does not touch the depths of his own imposture, the humorist will be sincere in spite of himself. Human beings are like machines, but machines too have souls; and if nature is only the first convention, the convention itself has become nature again. We can feel a heart beating tenderly within all these little beings of steel, fabric and porcelain.

Ravel's music expresses something, but only when it does not want to; it does not refute either the words of Stravinsky or Alain: 'Expression has never been the immanent property of music'.[1] Ravel is profound precisely because he is superficial; his profundity is as limpid as that of Vermeer or Terborch, and resides entirely in precision – it is the contrary of dialectical profundity. The lake into which Ondine dives is deep, says Roland-Manuel. So is the appearance that reveals to us, with the emptiness of false profundity, the crystalline depths of ingenuity. Ravel searched for this divine ingenuity under many different forms – among animals, for which his entire work, from the zoology of the *Histoires naturelles* onwards, proves his faithful affection, and most of all among children. For

---

[1] I. Stravinsky, *Chroniques de ma vie* I, p. 116. Alain, *Préliminaires a l'Esthétique*, p. 230: 'La musique n'exprime pas les passions, elle les efface'.

Ravel children were not what they were for Schumann, a metaphysical mystery, profound, earnest and almost too serious, but quite simply delightful anecdotes, signifying nothing beyond what they are: for it is the virtue of innocence to be profound by the mere fact of its presence, because it exists and not only because it represents the symbol of something else. In this way the Innocent in *Boris Godounov* utters prophecies without foresight. Profound innocence and learned simplicity – this is the only mystery about Debussy's Mélisande, and the greatest of all because precisely there is nothing to say about it. The mystery of Mélisande, and also that of her sister, the girl with the flaxen hair, the Mélisande of the north, the fairy of the reeds and heather – who is like her sister, fortunate but sad. It is the mystery of Mélisande and also of her Russian sister, the gentle Fevronia, Fevronia Mouromskaia, the very pure, the diaphonous being whose ingenuousness transfigures the sublime music of 'Kitezh, the Invisible City'. This is the end of the hermeneutical disguises; now everything is clear, virginal and perfectly translucid. An obscure purity. Yet even this transparency is won over an elementary primitiveness; for the little wild being of *L'Enfant et les sortilèges* bears no resemblance to the well-behaved doll in *Children's corner* working

At Le Havre, on return from U.S.A

at his *Gradus ad Parnassum*, and Fauré's Dolly plays with her elephant in a very western type of nursery; his destructive instinct brings him much closer to the little savages of Mussorgsky. If therefore 'the poet speaks' it is not in order to solve the riddle or decipher the hidden meanings of these games, but in order to show us the powers of passion transfigured by goodness. There are no secrets. In this Ravel comes nearer to the exquisite childhood songs of Anatole Liadov than the albums of Tchaikovsky. Indeed the Ravel of *Ma Mère l'oye*, the *Sonatine*, the *Noël des jouets* and most of all *L'Enfant et les sortilèges*, was able to amuse himself, like Debussy in the *Boîte à joujoux*, with the microscopic perspective that the eyes of a child give to things; for there is a miniature scale, an eye for the very small which makes details stand out and for which musical childhood or nursery suites easily afford pretexts: in *Le Festin de l'araignée* for example the ants see cats as big as elephants. The child is not a miniature adult. But there is some

thing else. The most wily artist of the whole world was also the most childish that could possibly be imagined; as childish as Dostoievsky's Prince Mishkin; enigmatic, silent and discreet as Mussorgsky's Incomprehensible; it looks as though this credulous, tiny conscience is only truly at his ease when in the company of nightingales, cockchafers, cats and children. Maurice Ravel also, like the virgin Fevronia, is like a nightingale. Amongst all the more or less suspect *gamineries* of the post-war period, among all the well-concerted forms of modern infantilism, Maurice Ravel represented innocence. And when he died our innocence died too.

'He groaned... I suffer and I bleed'. 'He suffers, he is wounded, he bleeds'. These two laments, one in *Le Martyre de Saint Sébastien*, the other at the end of *L'Enfant et les sortilèges*, express the same access of goodness; Debussy's

158

monody, harmonised with chords that are almost Ravelian in nature, and Ravel's almost Debussyist choir, whisper the same secret to us. 'The Child is good and gentle', sings the benevolent choir of animals, and these affectionate syllables irresistibly evoke the dawn scene from *Daphnis*. For finally such is the supreme message of innocence: gracious redemption through pity, the infinite value of a charitable instinct. And in the same way the metamorphosis of the Beast into Prince Charming signifies that a pure soul will be pardoned and that sincere love can beautify all ugliness. But Ravel would have been so afraid of being misunderstood that he would have blushed to admit it. Ravel therefore preferred to give the impression that he believed in nothing. But passionate tenderness reappears again in those melodies that look down like a modest glance, and one could say of them what Pierre Louijs said of the second *Chanson de Bilitis*: that one felt naked merely on listening to it. 'And he looked at me so tenderly that I shuddered and lowered my eyes'.

Chronology

These brief notes on the life and work of Ravel are entirely indebted to the indispensable books of Roland-Manuel and Hélène Jourdan-Morhange and to the correspondence collected by Marcelle Gérar and Réne Chalupt. Although they are necessarily sketchy, they cannot replace these books, and should encourage Ravel's admirers to discover him where he is most present – in the writings of those who knew him.

On the left-hand page will be found the list of his principal works and the description of the circumstances relating to them. On the right-hand page, Ravel speaks. We have borrowed from the Esquisse Biographique, *edited in October 1928 by Roland-Manuel from Ravel's dictation at the request of a firm of mechanical pianos, and published for the first time in the special number of* La Revue Musicale (*December 1938*). *These passages are followed by the note* (E.B.). *Apart from this all fragments from letters quoted (with the exception of one or two which belong to the book by Roland-Manuel) are taken from* 'Ravel, au miroir de ses lettres', *with the kind permission of its authors, whom we thank most sincerely.*

F.-R. B.

7th March 1875: Birth of Maurice Ravel, at Number 12, Quai de la Nivelle, now Quai Maurice-Ravel, at Ciboure, near Saint-Jean-de-Luz. His father, Joseph Ravel, engineer, is the inventor of a 'steam generator heated by mineral oils, applied to locomotion', and of the 'supercharged two-stroke engine'. The Ravel family originated from a village in Haute-Savoie. Joseph himself was born on the shores of Lake Léman. Called to Spain, after the war of 1870, to help with the building of railways, he met Maria Deluarte under the shady trees of Aranjuez and married her in 1874. The man from Savoie and the young Basque woman settled at Ciboure.

Ravel's mother.

'*At the age of three months, I left Ciboure for Paris, where I have lived ever since. As a small child I was sensitive to music – to every type of music. My father, who was better educated in this art than the majority of amateurs, knew how to develop my tastes and stimulated my zeal from an early date.*

Apart from tonic sol-fa, the theory of which I have never learnt, I began to study the piano at the age of about six. My teachers were Henri Ghys, then M. Charles René, from whom I had my first lessons in harmony, counterpoint and composition.

In 1889 I was admitted to the Paris Conservatoire in the preparatory piano class of Anthiôme, then, two years later, in that of Charles de Bériot. (E.B.)

161

Joseph Ravel and his two sons (on the left Edouard, on the right Maurice).

1891: first medal for piano. His best friend was Ricardo Viñes, who was to become one of his best interpreters. The two young students, enthusiastic about Chabrier's *Trois valses romantiques*, studied them and went to play them to the composer.

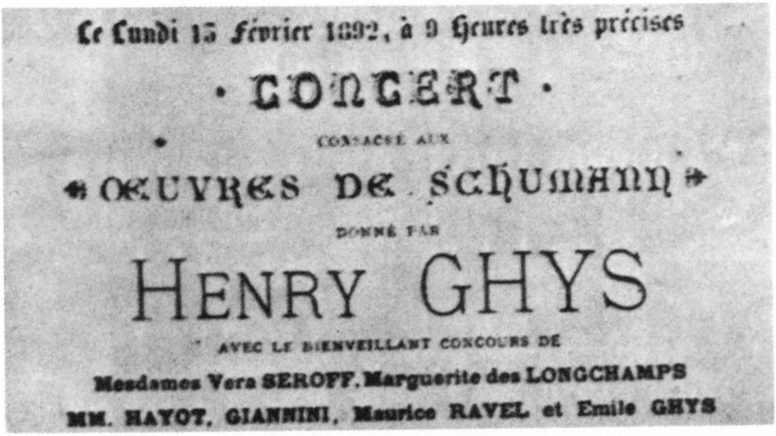

Ce Lundi 15 Février 1892, à 9 Heures très précises

· CONCERT ·

CONSACRÉ AUX

❀ OEUVRES DE SCHUMANN ❀

DONNÉ PAR

HENRY GHYS

AVEC LE BIENVEILLANT CONCOURS DE

Mesdames Vera SEROFF, Marguerite des LONGCHAMPS
MM. HAYOT, GIANNINI, Maurice RAVEL et Emile GHYS

1893: *Sérénade grotesque* (Chabrier's influence).

1894: *Ballade de la reine morte d'aimer* (influence of Erik Satie, whom Ravel met thanks to his father in the café La Nouvelle Athènes).

1895: At twenty, Ravel was a 'young man given to cynicism and reasoning, and somewhat distant, who read Mallarmé and visited Erik Satie' (Cortot). Ravel also read Baudelaire, Edgar Poe, Villiers de l'Isle-Adam and Condillac (at the same age, Stendhal was delighted by the same Condillac and his *Traité des Sensations*).

1897: Counterpoint and fugue class under the direction of André Gédalge and Gabriel Fauré's composition class (some years earlier, Debussy, in the same class, had had Massenet as teacher).

'*In 1895, I wrote my first published works:* the Menuet antique *and the* Habanera *for piano. I consider that this work contains the seed of several elements which were to predominate in my later compositions.* (E.B.)

One could not measure the importance of Fauré better than by studying his melodies which have enriched French music with the hegemony of lied. Forsaking the rigours of his teacher Saint-Saëns, Fauré was attracted even more by the undeniable colour of Gounod. Gounod, the true originator of melody in France, Gounod, who rediscovered the secret of a harmonic sensuousness lost since the harpsichordists of the XVIIth and XVIIIth centuries.

(Special number of the *Revue musicale* devoted to Fauré, 1923).

Fauré weaving the score of Pénélope (caricature by Losques).

27th May 1899: First hearing, under the direction of the composer, of the overture to *Shéhérazade* at the Société Nationale. Much booing and hissing. In the same year, *Pavane pour une infante défunte*.

1901: Ravel competed for the Prix de Rome for the first time and set to music a cantata by a M. Beissier called *Myrrha*. He received a second prize. Massenet tried to give him the first, which went to André Caplet.

The competitors for the Prix de Rome 1901: from right to left: Ravel, Bertelin, André Caplet, Aymé Kunc and Gabriel Dupont.

1902: *Quartet in F.* Debussy wrote to Ravel: 'In the name of the gods of music, and of mine, do not alter anything in your quartet'. On his side, Ravel confessed later to Mme. de Zogheb that 'it was as I was listening to *L'après-midi d'un faune* for the first time that I realised what music was.'

1902: Competition for the Prix de Rome. Cantata called *Alcyone*. M. Aymé Kunc received first prize.

164

'*It does not hurt when I talk about it, it is far enough back for the lapse of time to remove it from the composer to the critic. I can no longer see its qualities, from such a distance. But alas! I can very easily see its faults: the influence of Chabrier is too obvious, and the form rather poor. The remarkable playing of this incomplete and unpretentious work contributed largely, I think, to its success.*

Jeux d'eau, which appeared in 1901, was the origin of all the pianistic novelties which have been noticed in my work'. (E.B.)

'*After the appearance of* Pelléas et Mélisande (*the critics*) *placed themselves at the head of the Debussy supporters; from that moment they decided his ruin. The work was disturbing, they declared it sublime but exceptional. The word "dead end" was mentioned; then people waited. After that many young people decided to verify the affirmations of the critics, and discovered at the end of the "dead end" a door standing wide open on to a splendid and completely new type of country.*'

(Article appearing in the S. I. M. bulletin, Nov. 1912).

165

Portrait by Ouvré (1902).

Déodat de Séverac.

1903: Competition for the Prix de Rome. Cantata entitled *Alyssa*. M. Raoul Laparra receives first prize.

1904: Ravel decides not to enter the competition. He writes *Shéhérazade*, for voice and orchestra, based on poems by Tristan Klingsor.

1905: Competition for the Prix de Rome. Ravel is not even authorised to enter for the preliminary competition. A member of the musical section of the Institute declared: 'Monsieur Ravel may certainly consider us uninspired, but he won't take us for imbeciles with impunity...' The press denounced the scandal. It was called 'l'Affaire Ravel'. Romain Rolland himself protested energetically. Ravel, invited by his friends the Edwards (the director of *Le Matin*, the newspaper which at the same time welcomed the first short stories of Giraudoux), embarks on their yacht 'L'Aimée' for a cruise round Holland. The friendship saved Ravel from his discomfiture. Mrs. Edwards was born Misia Godebska and at that time the Godebskis, along with the Sordes, were the two centres for all Ravel followers: Léon-Paul Fargue, Maurice Delage, Roland-Manuel, Ingelbrecht, Déodat de Séverac, Falla, Florent Schmitt, La Fresnaye, Jean Cocteau, Valéry Larbaud, Georges Jean-Aubry, Stravinsky, Diaghilev, Nijinsky, etc... not forgetting a completely imaginary member of the 'company', Gomez de Riquet, who was talked of a great deal but never seen.

1905: *Miroirs*, pieces for piano (*Noctuelles, Oiseaux tristes, Une barque sur l'océan, Alborada del gracioso, La vallée des cloches*) and *Sonatine* for the piano. For some time Ravel thought of basing a dramatic fairy story on *Die Versunkene Glocke* by the German dramatist Gerhardt Hauptmann. Ravel lived with his family at 11 bis, rue Chevallier at Levallois-Perret, near the factory run by his brother Edouard.

'Yesterday we went to Alkmaar. Cheese market accompanied by a never-ending peal of bells. On the way, a most magnificent spectacle. A lake surrounded by windmills. In the fields, windmills right to the horizon. Wherever one looks, one can only see windmill sails turning. In the end one believes oneself automatic, because of the sight of this mechanical countryside. After all this, I don't need to tell you that I don't care about anything. But I am storing things up and I think that a great number of things will result from his trip. In any case, I am perfectly happy at the moment and I was very wrong to worry in a moment of gloom. You know how capable I am of taking things at their most tragic and, goodness me, there are worse'!

(Letter written on board 'L'Aimée', June 29th 1905, and addressed to Maurice Delage.

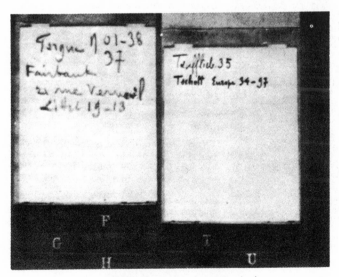

Ravel and Léon-Paul Fargue often telephoned each other...

1906: Journey round the shores of the Lake of Geneva, where Joseph Ravel was resting from the first attacks of an illness which proved fatal to him in 1908.

12th January 1907: First performance in the Salle Erard, of the *Histoires naturelles*, based on the poems of Jules Renard, in a fine uproar. The critic from 'Le Temps', Pierre Lalo, speaks of 'café-concert music with ninths'.

28th March 1908: First performance, at the Châtelet (Concerts Colonne) of the *Rhapsodie espagnole* (*Prélude à la nuit, Malagueña, Habanera, Feria*). The *Malagueña* is encored. 'The *Rhapsodie*', wrote Manuel de Falla, 'surprised me with its Spanish character. In perfect agreement with my own intentions (and quite opposed to those of Rimsky-Korsakov in his *Capriccio*), this hispanism was not achieved by simply copying popular music, but much more (with the exception of the *jota Feria*) by the free use of the rhythms, modal melodies and the ornaments of our popular compositions, which did not alter the author's own manner or the author...' *Revue musicale*, March 1939).

1907: *L'Heure espagnole*. After his librettist Franc-Nohain had listened to the score played on the piano, the latter merely said to Ravel: 'Fifty-six minutes'.

1908: *Ma Mère l'oye*, pieces for the piano dedicated to Mimie and Jean Godebski. *Gaspard de la nuit,* pieces for the piano, based on Aloysius Bertrand.

1911: *Valses nobles et sentimentales*. The epigraph is by Henri de Régnier: 'The delicious and perpetually novel pleasure of a useless occupation'.

168

'*The direct, clear language, the profound and hidden poetry in the plays of Jules Renard had attracted me for a long time. The very text imposed on me a particular style of declamation closely linked with the inflections of the French language. The* Histoires naturelles *prepared me for the composition of* L'Heure espagnole, *a lyrical comedy with book by M. Franc-Nohain, which is in itself a kind of conversation in music. My intention of joining up again with the tradition of the opéra-bouffe is affirmed here.* (E.B.)

The title of Valses nobles et sentimentales *indicates clearly enough my intention of composing a series of waltzes, following the example of Schubert. The virtuosity which formed the basis of* Gaspard de la nuit *is succeeded by a much clearer type of writing, which hardens the harmony and strengthens the musical reliefs. The* Valses nobles et sentimentales *were played for the first time among protests and hoots, at the "anonymous" concert of the S.M.I. The audience voted to name the composer of each item. The paternity of the* Valses *was attributed to me – with a small majority. The seventh seems to me the most characteristic.* (E.B.)

169

Illustration by Toulouse-Lautrec for 'Les Histoires naturelles'.

Décor for 'L'Heure espagnole'.

19th May 1911: First night at the Opéra-Comique of *L'Heure espagnole*, which had awaited M. Carré's decision for four years. Also in the programme, *Thérèse*, by Massenet. M. Pierre Lalo writes in *Le Temps*: 'His comedy is precious, dry and stiff, and does not let itself go freely for one moment... His characters lack life and soul as far as is possible...' and M. Emile Vuillermoz, in the review 'S.I.M.' wrote: 'In the name of logic, Ravel takes from musical language not only its internationality and its universality, but its simple humanity...'

Portrait by Ouvré (1911)

21st January 1912: Première at the Théâtre des Arts of the ballet adapted from *Ma Mère l'oye*.

22nd April 1912: Première at the Châtelet of the ballet *Adélaïde, ou le langage des fleurs*, taken from the *Valses nobles et sentimentales*. Ravel conducted the orchestra and confided to Roland-Manuel: 'It's not difficult, it's always in triple time... When his friend asked him what he did when duple and triple time were superimposed on each other, Ravel replied: 'At those places, I go round in circles'.

8th June 1912: Première, at the Châtelet, of the ballet *Daphnis et Chloé*, which Diaghilev ordered from Ravel, based on a plot by Fokine, choreographer of the Ballets Russes. Ravel began work in 1909 and finished on the 5th April, 1912. Nijinsky and Karsavina danced the principal rôles. Pierre Monteux conducted the orchestra. The décors were by Léon Bakst. The work was a real success, particularly during the year 1913. Later, M. Jacques Rouché included it in the repertoire of the Opéra. It is more often heard at concerts in the form of the well-known *Second Suite*.

Laideronnette's costume in 'Ma Mère l'oye. (L. Leyritz).'

Décor for the first act of 'Daphnis et Chloé' (Léon Bakst).

'*My intention in writing* Daphnis et Chloé *was to compose a vast musical fresco, less concerned with archaism than with fidelity to the Greece of my dreams, which is very similar to that imagined and depicted by the French artists at the end of the XVIIIth century.*' (E.B.)

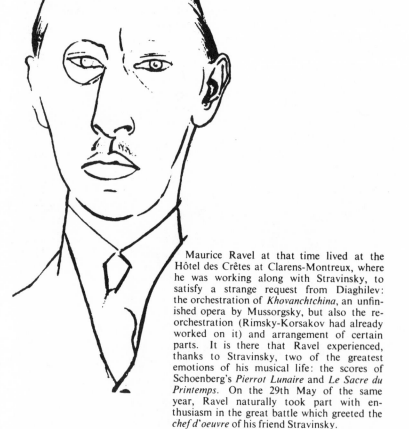

Stravinsky, by Picasso (1917).

Maurice Ravel at that time lived at the Hôtel des Crêtes at Clarens-Montreux, where he was working along with Stravinsky, to satisfy a strange request from Diaghilev: the orchestration of *Khovanchtchina*, an unfinished opera by Mussorgsky, but also the re-orchestration (Rimsky-Korsakov had already worked on it) and arrangement of certain parts. It is there that Ravel experienced, thanks to Stravinsky, two of the greatest emotions of his musical life: the scores of Schoenberg's *Pierrot Lunaire* and *Le Sacre du Printemps*. On the 29th May of the same year, Ravel naturally took part with enthusiasm in the great battle which greeted the *chef d'oeuvre* of his friend Stravinsky.

1913: *Trois poèmes de Stéphane Mallarmé*, for voice, piano, string quartet, two flutes and two clarinets.

'AT THE COMMITTEE OF THE S.M.I.: *Wonderful project for a scandalous concert:*

Pieces for a) *recitation,* b) *and* c) *voice and piano, string quartet, 2 flutes and 2 clarinets.*

    a)   Pierrot Lunaire, *Schoenberg (21 pieces, 40 minutes)*

    b)   Mélodies japonaises, *Stravinsky (4 pieces, 10 minutes)*

    c)   Two poems by S. Mallarmé, *Maurice Ravel.*

I assured Stravinsky that thanks to Ingelbrecht our choirs in France have been ruined for the singing of what he has composed lately, which is most difficult. Excellent for orchestral concert (very short, hardly 5 minutes).

Let independence hold you in her sacred keeping. But not too much so! Perhaps not in the Salle du Conservatoire. The ministers would not admit the same behaviour as in the Chambre des Députés.

(Letter to Mme. Alfred Casella, dated the 2nd April, 1913.)

Costumes for the little tree-frogs in 'L'Enfant et les sortilèges' (M. Terrasse).

Avenue Carnot (January 1913).

1914: The *Trio in A*, for piano, violin and cello, was entirely composed in 1914 at Saint-Jean-de-Luz, and one cannot hear it without feeling the luminosity of the Basque sky. At the same time, after the declaration of war, Ravel thought only of going to the front, in spite of the sadness he felt at leaving his mother. He increased his activity, but came up against the refusal of the military authorities at Bayonne; his small frame and his fragile appearance kept him away from armed service. The letters which he wrote to his friends in these moments are particularly moving.

176

At Ciboure, in front of the house where he was born (1914)

'*I work with open windows in spring weather. Occasionally a small cyclone, a shower the next day and then no more. Meanwhile I work for the benefit of the boss. You know that this august person, whose plans for costumes will soon be carried out by the firm of Redfern, has just launched a new dance, the* forlane. *I am transcribing one by Couperin*[1]. *I'm going to busy myself with having it danced at the Vatican by Mistinguett and Colette Willy in disguise. Don't be surprised by this return to religion. It's the native atmosphere that does it.*

There's the Angelus. I'm hurrying down to have dinner.

Dear friend, as you had foreseen, my adventure finished in the most ridiculous way: I'm not wanted because my weight is two kilograms short. Before going to Bayonne I spent one month working from morning till night, without even taking the time to bathe in the sea. I wanted to finish my Trio which I have treated as a posthumous work.

Evidentally an allusion to the *Forlane* in the future *Tombeau de Couperin*.

1915: *Trois chansons* for mixed choir without accompaniment. (*Nicolette, Trois beaux oiseaux du Paradis, Ronde*) to poems by Ravel. The second of these songs, dedicated to Roland-Manuel, who was in the Dardanelles, says particularly: My friend is away at the war... The third, *Ronde*, is of such rapid movement that one cannot catch the words; these can be found opposite.

14th March 1916: Ravel at last succeeded in obtaining the job of lorry driver. He is sent to Verdun. His address henceforth 'Driver Ravel – S.P. 4 par B.C.M.'

1916: Dysentery; an operation while at the front; transfer to the automobile park of Châlons-sur-Marne (6th September); reading of *Le Grand Meaulnes* by Alain Fournier: Ravel is impressed and from this moment thought of using this novel as inspiration for composing a work for cello and orchestra. *Adélaïde* was being danced at the Opéra, but driver Ravel had cold feet and waited until he had convalescent leave. His mother died on the 5th January 1917. Ravel spent a month in Paris, then left again for Châlons.

20th June 1917: Ravel settled at Lyons-la-Forêt, definitely reformed, and set to work again. The same day, he wrote to his friend Lucien Garban asking him to send him Liszt's *Transcendental Studies*.

1917: *Le Tombeau de Couperin*. These six pieces for piano, each one dedicated to a friend killed at the front, were orchestrated (with the exception of the *Fugue* and the *Toccata*) by Ravel for the Concerts Pasdeloup, and Jean Börlin's Ballets Suédois.

1919: Stay at Mégève, then at Lapras, near Lamastre (Ardèche). Diaghilev commissioned a choreographic poem from Ravel on the theme of Vienna and its waltzes. *L'Heure espagnole* performed in London (Covent Garden) and was a triumph (seventeen curtain-calls). Marguerite Long gave the first performance, in the Salle Gaveau, of *Le Tombeau de Couperin*.

Fire's costume from
'L'Enfant et les sortilèges'
(P. Colin).

That does not mean that I have lavished genius on it but that the order of my manuscript and of the notes concerning it would allow anybody else to correct the proofs. It is all useless: the result will only be another Trio . . .

(Letter to Ida Godebska dated the 8th September 1914)

N'allez pas au bois d'Ormonde
Jeunes filles, n'allez pas au bois.
Il y a plein de satyres, de centaures, de malins sorciers,
Des farfadets, des incubes, des ogres, des lutins,
Des faunes, des follets, des lamies, diables, diablots, diablotins,
Des chèvres-pieds, des gnomes, des démons, des loups-garous,
Des elfes, des myrmidons, des enchanteurs et des mages,
Des stryges, des sylphes et des moines bourrus, des cyclopes,
*   des djinns,*
Gobelins, korrigans, nécromants, kobolds . . . Ah!

(Ronde from the *Trois Chansons.* Poem by Ravel)

The major strongly advised me against aviation. I have hypertrophy of the heart. Oh! Not much, and it isn't serious, I was told. I wouldn't be concerned about it if I had a little heart trouble all my life as in the case of most men, but there: when at the end of last year I had myself properly examined, the doctors did not discover anything. Therefore it is accidental and I can explain to myself now this awful illness which my adventurous life prevented me from thinking about.

What should I do now? If I go through the inspection again before a more severe major, I will be declared unsuitable for driving and I'll be pushed into the offices. You will understand that I prefer to let things take their course. I shall not be the only one who has been side-tracked by the war. And then, what's more, I don't regret what I have done. If it is has only been declared lately, I know very well that it began on the 3rd August 1914 at three o'clock in the afternoon.

(Letter to Jean Marnold dated May 25th 1916).

179

16th January 1920: Promotion of M. Ravel, Joseph-Maurice, to the order of the Légion d'Honneur. Ravel telegraphed to Roland-Manuel at once imploring him to *deny it*, and obstinately refused to exercise his rights of chancery, which will cause it to be struck from *Le Journal Officiel*. The minister of Public Instruction, M. Léon Bérard, was most upset.

Several days earlier, *La Valse* was given a first hearing during the Concerts Lamoureux in the Salle Gaveau, under the direction of Camille Chevillard. Diaghilev had refused to stage this work.

15th June 1921: Ravel conducted the hundredth performance of the ballet taken from *Le Tombeau de Couperin* performed by the Ballets Suédois. He had just settled in at the 'Belvédère' at Montfort l'Amaury where he finished the Sonata for violin and cello, of which the first performance was to be given by Hélène Jourdan-Morhange and Maurice Maréchal.

Summer 1922: Orchestration, at Lyons-la-Forêt, near Roland-Manuel's home, of the *Pictures from an Exhibition* by Mussorgsky (at the request of Serge Koussevitsky).

1923: Journeys and concert tours to Amsterdam, Venice, London, where he conducted *La Valse* and *Ma Mère l'oye*. Ravel was very proud to be judged by the English *if not a great, at least a good conductor*. (Letter to Hélène Jourdan-Morhange of the 16th April 1923).

1924: Ravel worked simultaneously at the Sonata for violin and piano, at *Tzigane*, a virtuoso piece for violin and piano–luthéal, at a melody *Ronsard à son âme*, dedicated to Marcelle Gérar, and above all at *L'Enfant et les sortilèges*, undertaken in 1920, which had to be delivered to the Monte-Carlo Opéra before December 31st 1924.

He nevertheless went to Barcelona, for a concert devoted to his works, in the company of Marcelle Gérar. In a café a violinist recognised him and played the *Habanera*. Ravel thanked him and asked to hear some jazz. The violinist was amazed.

'*I sometimes think of an admirable convent in Spain, but, without faith, it would be completely mad. And how could I compose Viennese waltzes and other fox-trots there . . .*

(Letter to Mlle. Marnold dated March 25th 1920 at Lamastre).

After Le Tombeau de Couperin, *my state of health prevented me from writing for some time. I only started composing again for* La Valse, *a choreographic poem, which had first occurred to me before the* Rhapsodie espagnole. *I conceived this work as a kind of apotheosis of the Viennese waltz which is mingled, in my own mind, with the impression of a fantastic and fatal wild circling movement. I place this waltz in the background of an imperial palace; about 1855.* (E.B.)

I think that this Sonata marks a turning-point in the evolution of my career. Starkness has been carried to its extreme. Renunciation of harmonic charm; increasingly marked reaction in the sense of melody. (E.B.)

181

Frontispiece by Dufy for the works of Bartók, Dukas, Falla, Goossens, Malipiero, Ravel, Roussel, Schmitt, Satie and Stravinsky, which constitute the 'Tombeau' of Debussy; Ravel having written the Sonata for violin and cello specially.

Madeleine Grey.

Lunch at Montfort. From left to right: Mme. Delage, Gil-Marchex, Mme. Gil-Marchex, Mme. Ibert and Mme. Joaquin Nin. Arthur Honegger and Roland-Manuel dressed as cooks.

March 1925: First performance at Monte-Carlo of *L'Enfant et les sortilèges* under the direction of Victor de Sabata. M. Jacques Rouché had the honour of having given to Ravel, in 1917, the text by Colette entitled simply 'Ballet for my daughter'. Ravel asked his unexpected librettist for several revisions. 'He only seemed to worry', said Colette (in *Maurice Ravel*, Ed. du Tambourinaire) 'about the miaowing duet between the two cats, and seriously asked me if I found it inconvenient if he replaced *mouao* by *mouain*, or the contrary.'

1st February 1926: First performance in Paris (Opéra-Comique) of *L'Enfant et les sortilèges*, under the direction of Albert Wolff. Audience disconcerted. Criticism moderate. Fifteen performances. Ravel was on a concert tour in Scandinavia and England.

1926: *Chansons madécasses*, for voice, flute, cello and piano, this ensemble having been fixed by the 'backer' of the work, an American music-lover, Mrs. Elisabeth S. Coolidge. The first performances of these melodies were given successively by Madeleine Grey and Jane Bathori.

'*What would you think of the cup and teapot in old black Wedgewood singing rag-time? I admit that the idea of having rag-time sung by two negroes at the National Academy of music delights me.*'

(Letter to Colette)

The Chansons madécasses *seem to me to express a new dramatic element – perhaps erotic, which has been introduced into them by the very subject of Parny's songs. It is a kind of quartet where the voice plays the rôle of the main instrument. Simplicity dominates everything. The independence of the parts (affirms itself) and it will be found more marked in the Sonata. I imposed this independence upon myself and I wrote a Sonata for piano and violin, essentially incompatible instruments and which, far from balancing out their contrasts, here strengthen that incompatibility.* (E.B.)

183

Costume for the teacup in 'L'Enfant et les sortilèges' (P. Colin).

1927: Sonata for piano and violin, dedicated to Hélène Jourdan-Morhange.

1928: Tour of Canada and the United States, from New York to Chicago, from San Francisco to Los Angeles, Seattle, Vancouver, Minneapolis, Houston, Colorado, Buffalo, New York and Montreal. After one of the concerts, conducted by Koussevitsky, Ravel received an ovation of ten minutes, but obstinately refused to come on stage. Everywhere he conducted the orchestra, or played his *Sonatine*, or accompanied his songs. To Gershwin, who asked him for lessons, Ravel replied: 'You would lose the great spontaneity of your melody and you would only write bad Ravel.' (Reported by M. Goss, in *Boléro*.)

20th November 1928: First performance of the ballet *Boléro* at the Opéra by the Ida Rubinstein ballet, who had commissioned it several months earlier; Ravel had begun it at Saint-Jean-de-Luz. Gustave Samazeuilh writes in *La Revue musicale* (1938): I enjoyed the rich spectacle of seeing Ravel in a yellow bathing-wrap and red cap, playing to me, before we went to take our morning dip, the theme of *Boléro*, and saying to me: 'Mme. Rubinstein has asked me for a ballet. Don't you find that this theme is persistent? I'm going to try to repeat it again several times with no development, graduating my orchestra as best I can.' At the première, a lady, clutching her seat, cried: 'He's mad! He's mad!' Ravel, to whom his brother recounted the scene, added: 'She has understood!' M. José Bruyr also reports in his 'Maurice Ravel' this statement by the composer concerning his best-known work: 'Once the idea was found, any student from the Conservatoire would, as far as that modulation, succeed as well as I have done'.

September 1929: The rue du Quai, at Ciboure, becomes the quai Maurice-Ravel.

1929–1931: Simultaneous composition of the two Concertos, Ravel dividing his time between Levallois, Montfort and long evenings

At the Belvedere, from left to right and from top to bottom: Andrée Vaurabourg, Mme. Lucien Garban, Arthur Honegger, Germaine Tailleferre, Mme. X, Madeleine Picard, Lucien Garban, Ravel and Mlle. Pavloski.

In the U.S.A. with Mary Pickford and Douglas Fairbanks.

A. Durand & Fils Éditeurs　　Paris.　31/I　1929

DURAND & Cⁱᵉ

4 Place de la Madeleine

Paris

Monsieur Maurice RAVEL
Montfort l'Amaury

Cher Monsieur,

Nous avons l'avantage de vous remettre,
ci-inclus, à valoir sur travaux en cours, la
somme de Cinq cents francs, en cinq billets de
banque de cent francs, montant de votre mensua-
lité de Janvier.

with his friends. The Concerto for the Left Hand, written at the request of the Austrian pianist Wittgenstein, whose right arm had been amputated, was finished and performed first in Vienna on November 27th 1931. The *Concerto in G*, was first performed in Paris at the Salle Pleyel, on the 14th January 1932, Marguerite Long at the piano, Ravel conducting the orchestra. Immediately afterwards Ravel undertook a big tour in Central Europe, with Marguerite Long, to play this Concerto, with immense success everywhere.

1932: *Don Quichotte à Dulcinée* (words by P. Morand), voice and piano. Ravel has nothing but projects: to base a great lyrical work on Delteil's Jeanne d'Arc; a fairy story, *Morgiane*, from the 'Story of Ali Baba': a symphonic work based on 'Le Grand Meaulnes', an oratorio based on 'The Little Flowers of St. Francis'. Manuel de Falla even states (*Revue musicale*, 1938) that one of the parts, the 'Sermon to the Birds', had been drafted.

1933: First attack of illness; bathing at Saint-Jean-de-Luz, Ravel notices that he can no longer make certain movements. He leaves for a rest at Mont-Pèlerin, near Vevey. The doctors taek of apraxia and dysphasia. Ravel's mind is perfectly clear. He is only incapable of writing, even of reaching an object near at hand. At Montfort, where Hélène Jourdan-Morhange found him leaning on his balcony, and asked him what he was doing, Ravel replied: *I'm waiting.*

15th February 1935: Departure, with his great friend Léon Leyritz, and thanks to Mme. Ida Rubinstein, for a fabulous voyage to Spain and Morocco. Embarkation at Algeciras, after a night in Madrid. Three weeks in Marrakech, at the Hôtel de la Mamounia. Ravel spends hours contemplating the spectacle of the Place Djemma-el-Fna. The Glaoui gives fêtes in his honour. Si Mammeri makes him hear Moroccan airs of the XVIth century. Excursion to Telouët, in the Atlas mountains, domain of one of the Glaoui's sons. The garden

Ravel as Doctor 'honoris causa', Oxford (1931).

A game of pelota at Saint-Jean-de-Luz.

This card brings you my best wishes and a few vague details about the state of my fillies: Concerto I, Concerto II, Daedalus VI (outsider). I am even less decided about the rating of this last one than Giraudoux was about his Amphitryon.

(Letter to Madame Kahn-Casella, dated, 27 th December, 1929)

187

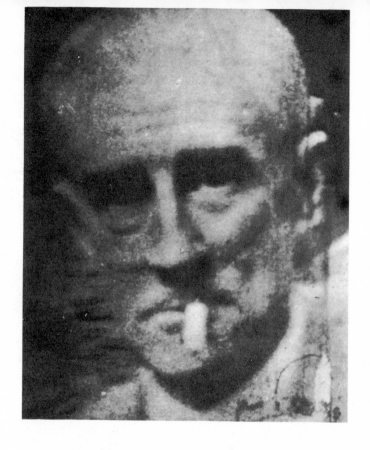

of the Oudayas, near Fez. Return via Seville and Cordoba, Vittoria and Pampeluna.

1936–1937: At Saint-Jean-de-Luz or at Montfort, at Levallois, near his brother or in Paris with his friend Maurice Delage, Ravel lives quietly, surrounded by his friends, cared for by his faithful housekeeper Mme. Révelot.

19th December 1937: Operation by Professor Clovis Vincent at the clinic in the Rue Boileau.

28th December, in the early hours, death of Maurice Ravel, who was buried in the cemetery at Levallois, near his parents.

Musical examples

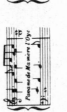

Daphnis

Pavane de Ma mère l'Oye

Adagio du Concerto en sol

Trois beaux oiseaux du Paradis

CADENCES

Daphnis

Daphnis

Daphnis

L'Enfant et les Sortilèges

AOUA

STRING QUARTET

1er Mouvement

Scherzo

Andante

Finale

SONATE EN DUO

A selected discography from Great Britain and America

PIANO MUSIC

Gaspard de la Nuit
Robert Casadesus   Philips ABL 3046 (G.B.)   Columbia ML 4519 (U.S.A.)
Miroirs
* *Robert Casadesus*   Philips ABL 3012 (G.B.)
Gieseking   in Angel 3541-5 (Set) (U.S.A.)
Pavane pour une Infante défunte
Robert Casadesus   Philips ABL 3012 (G.B.)
Gieseking   in Angel 3541-5 (set) (U.S.A.)
Sonatine
Kathleen Long   Decca LK 4043 (G.B.)
Gieseking   in Angel 3541-5 (set) (U.S.A.)
Le Tombeau de Couperin
Kathleen Long   Decca LK 4043 (G.B.)
Gieseking   in Angel 3541-5 (set) (U.S.A.)
Valses nobles et sentimentales
Friedrich Gulda   Decca LXT 5415 (G.B.)
Gieseking   in Angel 3541-5 (set) (U.S.A.)

CONCERTOS

Concerto in G for piano and orchestra
Michelangeli and the Philharmonia/Ettore Gracis   HMV ALP 1538 (G.B.)
Blancard and Orchestra Suisse Romande/Ansermet London LL 797 (U.S.A.)
Concerto for Left Hand, piano and orchestra
Blancard and Orchestra Suisse Romande/Ansermet
Decca LXT 2814 (G.B.)   London LL 797 (U.S.A.)

VOCAL

Shéhérazade (for voice and orchestra)
Suzanne Danco with Orchestra Suisse Romande/Ansermet Decca LXT 5031 (G.B.)
Tourel, Columbia Symphony Orchestra/Bernstein   Columbia ML 4289

---

* Walter Gieseking and Robert Casadesus have both recorded Ravel's complete piano works. These are available in Great Britain and America.

CHAMBER MUSIC

Introduction and Allegro for Harp, Flute, Clarinet and strings
Hollywood Quartet, Stockton, Gleghorn. Lurie
Capitol CCL 7509 (G.B.)   Capitol P 8304 (U.S.A.)
String Quartet in F
Loewenguth Quartet   Deutsche Gramophon DG 16073 (G.B.)
Stuyvesant Quartet   Philharmonia 104 (U.S.A.)
Trio in A Minor
Rubinstein, Heifetz, Piatigorsky   HMV ALP 1009 (G.B.)
Albeneri Trio   Mercury 10089 (U.S.A.)
Sonata for Violin and Piano
Dervy Erlih, M. Bureau   Ducretet-Thomson Dtl 93106 (G.B.)
Francescatti, Balsam   Columbia ML 5058 (U.S.A.)
Tzigane
Ginette and Jean Neveu   HMV ALP 1520 (G.B.)
Francescatti, Balsam   Columbia ML 5058 (U.S.A.)

ORCHESTRAL

Boléro
Paris Opéra Orchestra/Rosenthal   Aurora aab 112 (G.B.)
Philadelphia Orchestra/Ormandy   Columbia ML 5257 (U.S.A.)
Daphnis et Chloé (complete)
Paris Opéra Orchestra/Rosenthal   Aurora aab 111 (G.B.)
Orchestra Suisse Romande/Ansermet   London LL 693 (U.S.A.)
Daphnis et Chloé, suite 2
Philharmonia Orchestra/Cantelli   HMV ALP 1089 (G.B.)
Philadelphia Orchestra/Ormandy   Columbia ML 4316
Rhapsodie Espagnole
Paris Opéra Orchestra/Rosenthal   Aurora aab 113 (G.B.)
Boston Symphony Orchestra/Munch   Victor LM 1984 (U.S.A.)
La Valse
Paris Opéra Orchestra/Rosenthal   Aurora aab. 114 (G.B.)
Boston Symphony Orchestra/Munch   Victor LM 1700 (U.S.A.)
Valse nobles et sentimentales
Paris Opéra Orchestra/Rosenthal   Aurora aab 113 (G.B.)
Orchestra Suisse Romande/Ansermet   London LL 795 (U.S.A.)
Le Tombeau de Couperin
Paris Opéra Orchestra/Rosenthal   Aurora aab 114 (G.B.)
Orchestra Suisse Romande/Ansermet   London LL 795 (U.S.A.)
Ma Mere l'oye
Paris Opéra Orchestra/Rosenthal   Aurora aab 112 (G.B.)

OPERA

L'Enfant et les sortileges
Flore Wend, Suzanne Danco, Motet choir of Geneva, Orchestra Suisse Romande/Ansermet   Decca LXT 5019 (G.B.)   London A-4105 (U.S.A.)
L'Heure Espagnole
Denise Duval, Orchestra Opéra Comique/Cluytens
Columbia 33 CX 1076 (G.B.)   Angel 35018 (U.S.A.)

Selected bibliography

Three indispensable books

ROLAND-MANUEL: *Maurice Ravel* (revised edition, Gallimard, 1948). English translation by C. Jolly (Dobson, London, 1947)

HÉLÈNE JOURDAN-MORHANGE: *Ravel et nous* (Ed. du Milieu du Monde, 1945)
RENÉ CHALUPT: *Ravel au miroir de ses lettres*, correspondence selected by Marcelle Gérar and René Chalupt (Ed. Robert Laffont, 1956)

Also worth consulting

ROLAND-MANUEL: *Ravel et son oeuvre dramatique* (Ed. Librairie de France, 1928)
Special number of 'La Revue musicale', *Hommage à Maurice Ravel* (December, 1938)

COLETTE, L-P FARGUE, M. DELAGE, TRISTAN KLINGSOR, ROLAND-MANUEL, D. SORDET, E. VUILLERMOZ and J. DE ZOGHEB: *Maurice Ravel* (Ed. du Tambourinaire, 1939)

MARGUERITE ⁄ LONG, HÉLÈNE JOURDAN-MORHANGE, TONY AUBIN, ARTHUR HOÉRÉE, L-P FARGUE and G. PIOCH: *Maurice Ravel* (Publications Techniques et Artistiques, 1945)

FRANK ONNEN: *Maurice Ravel* (English translation, Continental Book Company, A.B., Stockholm, 1947)

ARMAND MACHABEY: *Maurice Ravel*, Collection 'Triptyque', ed. Richard-Masse (Plon, 1950)

Of special interest to pianists:

HÉLÈNE JOURDAN-MORHANGE and VLADO PERLEMUTER: *Ravel d'après Ravel* (Ed. du Cervin, Lausanne, 1953)

ICONOGRAPHY

Marcelle Gérar's collection: pp. 20, 137, 158, 182, 185
Hélène Jourdan-Morhange's collection: pp. 53, 59, 83, 89, 97, 188
Léon Levritz's collection: pp. 112, 124, 143, 147, 149, 187
Roland-Manuel's collection: pp. 2, 39, 161, 162, 184
Lipnitzki: pp. 75, 90, 91, 138
Roger Roche: pp. 24, 66, 68, 73, 77, 79, 80, 123, 126, 131, 160, 167, 168, 180
George-Jean Aubry's collection: p. 33
Ariel-Temporal Photos: p. 41
Sextia-Aude Photos: p. 121
Harlingue: pp. 176, 177
Wide World: p. 186
Etienne Photos, Bayonne: pp. 3 and 3 of inside cover
The costume drawings were provided by the Paris Opera Library.

DATE DUE

DEMCO 38-297